THE HA-HA

JANNIFER DAWSON

Dawson, Jennifer   61-26144
    The ha-ha.   [London]
A. Blond [1961] $3.75

MAIN

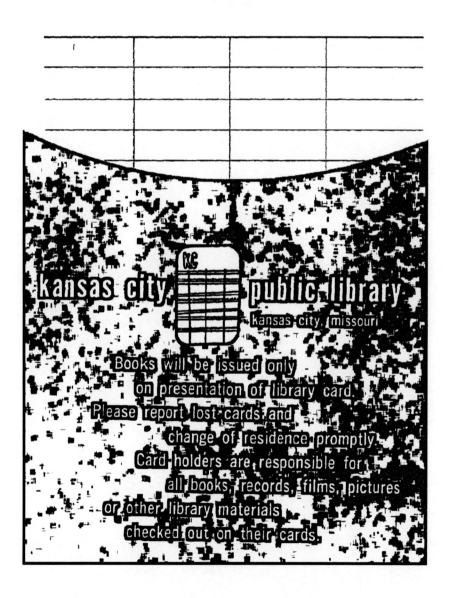

DAY

THE HA-HA

The Ha-Ha

Jennifer Dawson

Boston - Toronto

LITTLE, BROWN AND COMPANY

Little Fly
Thy summer's play
My thoughtless hand
Has brush'd away.

Am I not a fly like thee?
Or art thou not a man like me?

BLAKE

Chapter One

'THEY WERE all very kind at Oxford,' I assured her, for she had seemed to think they were not. 'No one shunned me or ripped my stockings or took my bicycle on "loan".'

'So,' said the Sister nodding as she slid the enormous bundle of silver keys into her pocket. 'So. That was good.'

She smiled and waited for me to go on. She was a German, I thought. Her voice moved up and down so, and her 'r's were so rich and long in her throat.

'So.' It seemed the right occasion, that first day, to go on. 'So you see, I could not have been unhappy there. In fact I had no enemies at all. The other students were all very friendly and pleasant, and used to wave as they passed and cry: "How goes it?" or "Press on regardless". Most encouraging. But in fact I never needed any encouragement. My favourite hymn had always been

"Glad that I live am I", to which Mother could add an excellent little alto part.'

'Really. Is that so?' the Sister nodded again, folding her starched apron carefully up in front of her and sitting down on the wireworks of the bed. I had not had time to make it up yet. 'May I? May I make myself at home? So. That was good.'

She had only just come in and introduced herself as the ward-sister, and I had only just moved up here, to the second floor, to the 'side-rooms', as they were called, from the other ward that was always full and noisy. The room was very small, like a cupboard, with an iron bed-stead down one half, and a wicker chair and a door on the other. It was a change of view I had only just been given, and when the Sister folded up her apron and sat down, I saw that the room was now mine, and that she wanted to talk.

'So, that was good,' she was repeating. She leaned back against the bed-end and stared at me. She was small and dark, but her eyes were large, and so full of a devouring emotion that I thought she might swallow me. 'The intellectual, academic world must have been a very great experience. In Germany we call it *studenten* . . .'

But I have forgotten now what she said they called it. For that was a year ago and my mind was full of other things then, surprise and expectation.

It was true though that Oxford had been a very great experience. You see, in my adolescence and at school I had never really been *au fait*. I used to get into trouble for thinking of the wrong things and letting them loose verbally, and as no one ever told me what the right ones were, I was in the dark most of the time. But at the University, I discovered, there was no rule of this kind. You were allowed to think of what you liked, without any hindrance.

The Sister leaned over and searched my face with her yearning eyes. 'So,' she cried, 'I see that you made some good friends at that very famous chair of learning? You ...' she fumbled for the word, 'you ...'

While she searched for the word I climbed over the bed on to the window-sill to see what it was like – this new world that I had just been given. It was evening. From the ward beneath came that prolonged, even and rhythmic clapping that I was so familiar with. I could picture her so well, Mrs. Dale, standing by the linen-room door in the twilight of the dark green corridor, clapping and applauding no one in particular, while the nurses picked up their aprons and handed in their keys. I remembered too how stuffy it had been in the evenings, and how my hopes would rise when the evening hymn started up, and the curtains were drawn across, and the night nurses started to arrive.

'So, you made some fertile friendships at the University?' the Sister pressed, rearranging her words tenaciously. 'You found a rich inheritance?' she pursued. 'Then perhaps when you leave here ...? to pick up the threads ...?'

No. I had not made any friends, even there. For apart

from Helena, who would drop in for a hot milk-drink in the evenings, and bring the 'Battle of Maldon' for some translation (which she was not very strong on) I had never been caught up in the student world.

I used to envy them though, as they shouted across the Broad, waving from their bicycles as though they did not mind about the ungulates and the horned mammals having been there before them – got there first, so to speak. I used to envy them as they called down from top windows in Walton Street, or spoke across the library-desk:

'Are you playing tennis this afternoon, Jane?' and the reply would come 'pat' before I had even had time in my mind's eye to string the racket so that the ball did not slip straight through the frame; while I was still wondering whether it was really cat-gut:

'Sorry, I've got an essay-crisis.'

I had often tried to describe Oxford life to Mother. I would tell her how they dressed and spent their time. I used to describe college balls and essay-crises and after-noons on the river and vacation trips and coffee-parties when they would stay up till midnight talking; I told her about how they sometimes fell in love or got engaged, and Mother would say that it took all types to make a world and that she would not like her student daughter to become too 'fast', to which I would agree.

I once said I thought they were like good riders who never came off their mounts, and she reminded me that we need more than one spill in life if it was to be a rich

one and a good one. To which I agreed. Mother smiled
and said her girl had plenty of imagination.

'Why do you not, one day, when "the moil" (meaning
my final examinations) is over, "when the battle's lost or
won",' she said playfully, 'try to write some little sketches
about Oxford life and personalities and your college
idols, remembering all sides of the picture . . .'

No, I had not made any firm friendships, even there.

'You see, unfortunately,' I tried to explain to the Sister,
'unfortunately I did not seem able to learn exactly how
the appropriate reply fitted on to the prior remark, and a
lot seemed to depend on this in undergraduate circles.
With me the two never seemed to dovetail.'

There had always been that strange hiatus, that funny
in-between gulf that other things took possession of
when you were off your guard, and surprised you
unawares: the purple buddleia with the butterfly clinging,
the kangaroo, the groves of spotted bananas, and the
egg-eating snake with the enamelled prong in his throat
(for piercing the shell with). They had always been there,
these other things, and when the undergraduates spoke
again or stood there waiting for me to affix the right
reply, I was, if you see what I mean, a little flummoxed,
a little behindhand; not quite up to the mark. I had been
tapped on the shoulder, so to speak; I seemed to be
reduced to silence by the things the others got round so
easily.

And then the laughter came. For when they spoke
again, those members of Oxford University with whom

I consorted, I could only laugh. Gale fumbling with the
zip of her evening gloves; Prue pouting over her make-
and-mend or struggling with the little portable wireless.
And outside were all these strange things, spotted or
quilled or feathered.

'It was because of all the other things,' I explained to
the Sister, 'that I usually ended in laughter.'

Unfortunately, it did not go unnoticed, and one day at
the Principal's little termly tea-party for her third-year
students, the laughter happened once too often.

She was pouring out tea, and one of the guests, a Miss
Veronica Piercy, was discussing the yearly 'Mission' to
the University.

'I am afraid, Lady Stocker,' she was saying, 'that we
are drifting near to a spiritual holocaust. Much as I
admire these Aldermaston Marchers, and racial demon-
strators, they surely tend to forget that in spite of all the
material threats to our valuable Western contribution to
civilization, a much graver one lies ahead in the form of a
spiritual waste, a spiritual vacuum. For the blank apathy
of the masses . . .'

There we all were, in a row on a striped Regency
settee, in afternoon dresses – Miss Piercy's was a pale
violet mohair – passing the painted, transparent cups and
the daintily rolled sandwiches that had been set before us.
Lady Stocker nodded politely, and another guest cried
with a great rush of approval:

'Oh! Lady Stocker, I couldn't agree more.'

As we sat there I could see the even-toed ungulates

marching through the waste, and files of armadillos with scaly shells, and hosts of big black flies. The door opened ... it was only the maid in a starched cap carrying the silver kettle, but the laugh I gave shocked even the Principal.

The animals ... the animals ... I wanted to tell them all about the animals, but would they understand? They say the English are great animal lovers. I don't think this can be strictly true though. I supposed at least that I was a great animal lover; that is how I explained my laughter when the Principal summoned me afterwards and suggested that I saw a specialist. I could just never get them out of my mind at Oxford. They were always there, the things of the jungle, making their appearance 'when one or two people were gathered together'.

I suppose they thought I was laughing at them, and I did not always have time to take them aside and explain why I was laughing; consequently, I didn't make many friends. Mother used to explain to her friends when they supposed that life at the 'Varsity must be a gay whirl of social activity, that I found them all rather thin; rather peripheral and light weight. That I 'ran through them all rather swiftly'. But as you can see, this was not strictly true, and as I did not like deceiving Mother or her friends, I should like to have taken them aside and explained why it was that life was not for me (though it was for some people), a 'gay round of social activity'.

'Excuse me,' my hand went to my mouth apologetically. 'Excuse me; I seem to have made rather a long speech about a very trivial story.'

I was surprised at it, but the Sister seemed interested. 'Go on,' she said.

'Nothing. Nothing else.'

'Nothing? Is that all? And have the animals retreated?' I nodded.

'Good,' she laughed approvingly, stopped abruptly, and stared thoughtfully ahead.

'When one is adolescent,' she began, appealing to me with her dark, sympathetic eyes, 'when one is adolescent, one often gets caught up in one's thoughts and dreams. That does sometimes happen to many of us. But,' she leaned over and tapped my hand playfully, 'you are no longer adolescent. That is all over now.'

It was all over, Oxford, the students, the Principal, the animals, and Mother's friends. It was all the past. It was all ancient history.

'Look at the geraniums,' I pointed them out, lolling in the big central bed in front of the main hospital doors. My window looked down over the drive that ran round the bed to the massive stone Gothic entrance hall. The cats were stalking round the few remaining cars, and someone, a man, was pacing up and down, bending over to light a cigarette, and stopping at the main door to talk to some invisible person within.

It was evening, and the broken piano was starting up down below. I could picture them standing round, shuffling through the hymn book for 'Jesu Lover of My

Soul' before the lights went on and the night came. Soon the woman in red who always stood at the window would be delivered of her baby and would be rocking it up and down to the stars instead of wringing her hands. And there beyond the drive and the pine trees and the high grey hospital wall was the hill, parched and yellowing and solitary, that Judas Iscariot and I used to peer at carefully every evening.

I pointed it out to the Sister.

'We used to stand there every evening in the dormitory staring at it.'

Judas would pick out the Gaumont tower with her spy-glass, and the rusty sheets of iron on the waste-patch, the ice-cream van, and the children sliding and riding pram-wheels down the slope. But we always came back to the hill. It was our religion.

Then one night when we were standing there as usual, I saw in a kind of preview that Judas was going to sigh and shut her grey melancholy eyes and start her poem: 'There is a green hill far away without a city wall.' And the terror would come to me: those final jumbled, confused lines that left me trembling, but which seemed to satisfy her so deeply:

'And now I wish the passing night had borne my breath away.'

But that day it was different, because I suddenly saw that if I shifted a little, if only I moved slightly, the dormitory would break up like a kaleidoscope pattern, and she would no longer be Judas Iscariot at all, and I would no longer have to be sitting there among the rows of iron beds with the pink plastic pots underneath.

The Sister blinked and smiled, and understood. 'So you flew away.' Her voice modulated sharply. 'I think that was good. And so you flew away like a bird out of a snare ... a snare such as the foresters make in the country where I come from, of damp black twigs.'

A trumpet came from the barracks. The night nurses began to cycle up the drive. The sun had disappeared behind the hill. I knew it would soon be dark. But night was no longer an ally as it had been then, when the air grew stuffy and the electric lights would click out until there was only one small circle of light in the middle of the rows of beds, and the nurses would shuffle to and fro round this island bringing you paraldehyde, that stung your eyes and throat and tasted of seaweed and the dark bottom of the sea.

It was good, this night, and I used to think that if there were a God, he was a God of darkness, and that day was just what happened to be left over for men to do what they liked in.

'And so . . .' The Sister broke abruptly into my thoughts. She rose and smoothed her apron back over her dark cotton dress. 'That is all over.' She was suddenly firm and rather severe, as though she had listened too much for too long. 'The past is a dream that is over, and one looks to the future to see what is there.' She emphasized the past and the future as though we were all Eurydices who must not look back.

I examined my brown and green mottled room. I thought about the future.

'Then I suppose I shall be leaving quite soon, now that I am better?' Only there was the problem that I did not know where to go now that Mother was dead. She had married rather late, and by the end there had only been the two of us at our house in Wookens Walk.

'Dearie.' The Sister sat down again. 'Nothing is thought *that* far yet. For the moment, tell me, can you regard this as your home? Can you? You must be working before we think of anything else.'

Work? I did not know anything to work at. At College I had specialized in Anglo-Saxon and become interested in the *Ormulum*. I described that ancient poem to her. 'I was very keen on that.'

But she did not know it: she was still very ignorant of English literature and hoped I would teach her. But she thought it more likely that for the moment a suitable form of work could be found through the social worker. It was the P.S.W.'s job, I learned, to 'place' people, to see them on to their feet in the real world.

'But it is real here,' I protested, at the window, pointing it out to her. I wanted to remain here at the window looking out on to the beds of geraniums, and the hot gardens, and the ward opposite where I could see them moving about.

'What is that block on the other side?'

'That is the male side of the hospital.'

'And what is that like?'

She was doubtful. She was not interested. 'Like this, more or less.' She began fidgeting with her note-books.

I peered. It seemed like this one, across the drive, except that where our windows had looked on to the bare airing-court, their view was unblocked. I could see men walking about in its day-room, and at the windows two boys, and an old man in a black beret crouched on a chair clutching something. At intervals in between them glided the white-coated figures of the male nurses.

'As soon as you are working,' the Sister was repeating, 'as soon as you have flown from under the leaves, back to the busy sky . . .' she laughed triumphantly at the metaphor . . . 'Is it good . . . ? we will only then start worrying about the future. When the committee have regraded you.'

The committee? Regrade? I knew they graded eggs and milk, I did not know that they also had this word for humans. 'Regrade me? . . . As what?'

'You came under certificate,' she brought out with a sigh as though she were repeating a lesson she was tired of. 'Why should that make any difference or upset anything?' She waited with pursed lips. She waited. 'Why should it, dearie?'

'Why?' I repeated mechanically without seeing quite what she meant, or what she was waiting to see upset.

Her eyes were half-closed as though she were praying. 'You are not frightened of labels, are you dearie? If you had come here because of some injury to your leg or arm you would not be made miserable by . . .'

But I was not miserable. I could assure her of that. I had escaped from the other ward; I had escaped from the fowler's snare, had I not, I asked myself. And besides that, the sun had shone for two months and it had not rained once. The nights were hot. The walls were hot when you walked near them. The grass was brown with it, like tobacco, and the leaves creaked with dryness when the birds touched them. The sunshine had become a kind of habit. I wanted to walk out there where for so many months I had only stared, and forget about the barren peach tree of the airing-court, and the well-beaten paths. I could not have been miserable then, even if there had been anything.

'It is grey with drought,' I noticed, 'and on the other side . . . ?'

'What dearie?' The Sister adjusted her glasses.

'The hill,' I pointed out. 'The Green Hill Far Away.'

'Ah yes, the hill.' She folded them up again with a snap. 'It wants a drink.'

We talked. She told me she had escaped from Munich in 1938 with other non-Aryans, and Munich she had been very fond of. She described the city, her home, her parents, her father. Her voice rose higher and higher. She blinked away the tears.

She smiled and I smiled. 'I'm sorry,' I said.

'Dearie,' she cried and clasped her hands over my knees and shook them. 'In Germany we have a phrase, a proverb, which means that one passes from knowledge to ignorance and there life begins. That is where I was once; that is where you are now, yes?'

There were heavy footsteps at the other end of the corridor. She leaped to her feet. 'Dr. Clements! Don't sit there dreaming on the window-sill or he will decide you are withdrawn and preoccupied and not ready for...' I was afraid she was going to say 'the real world'. But instead she said, 'a working day'.

At the door she turned back smiling.

'I am glad of my new patient . . . Shall we say, my new, most sympathetic neighbour? I think my ward will be richer for her, and I think sometimes I shall want to drop in here for a talk about life. In the meantime, I must run, and you must be patient till we find the right medium for you to flourish in when you are regraded.'

'How about the wild life round Munich,' I asked her. 'The badgers, for example, did they flourish?'

'I was always too short-sighted to see any,' she replied gaily.

She was gone. I went back to the window and stared at the heavy grey-green of the hospital entrance, and the electrically illuminated sign that had just clicked on over the door: 'Gardenwell Park.'

I had not acknowledged it until they had whisked me away from the dormitory, trailing my goods in a blanket, half an hour ago. I had thought of the hospital simply as a kind of net that encircled my mind as well as my body: that always seemed to stretch just a little farther than I could think, and to extend just a little farther than I could run when I wanted to escape. I had never thought much about its name or its exterior or what went on outside the green dormitory walls.

The block opposite was only a heavy dark smudge among the trees. The curtains had been pulled across its dayroom windows, and nothing was alight now except the name over the doors and the gleaming white of the gravel drive.

The Sister's footsteps were pattering fainter and fainter beside the Doctor's, and her voice was shrill beside his. A key tinkled, a door slammed. The hymn had stopped; so had the applause. There was silence; it spread round me in wider and wider circles as I sat there by the rickety shutters watching the fluttering stars.

How well I remember that first night! It was all so clear then, as though I had woken after a dream to see a dazzling light on the ceiling, and had run out to find that thick snow had fallen in the night, and everything was changed and new; as though I were about to run laughing out into all that whiteness.

'A month or so,' the Sister had said. But a month did not seem a very long time. I was already awakened and free, and the rest did not seem a matter of importance at all.

Chapter Two

IT WAS a matter of indifference to me that, as they had promised, they found me a job in the outside world. It was they, the Sister, the Doctor and the social worker who talked about getting back to the 'real world' as though there were two; one good and one to be avoided. To me it did not seem as though there were these two, and I would have been as pleased if instead of handing me back my private clothes and giving me town-parole, and money for lunches and bus fares, the authorities had left me to wander round the grounds all day, explore what lay beyond, or just to gaze out of my side-room window on to the other side of the hospital where everything was unfamiliar.

Yet when I had been 'placed' I found to my surprise that nothing had changed; my glass was as full and I was as happy as before. The place they had found was the house of a retired colonel and his wife. They had just come back from India and had settled in the town that lay beneath the ramparts of Gardenwell Park, and were looking for some temporary person to catalogue their books and arrange them into a small library.

I would arrive punctually at the tall Victorian house, and make my way speedily upstairs to the top floor where they had arranged a table and chair among the tea-chests, stacks of books, and old furniture, and if I cannot say I worked as punctiliously as my arrival suggested, that was only because the table was too near the window and gave me a view over the town, and because so many of Colonel Maybury's books dealt with the flora and fauna of the Asian continent.

It was a good life while it lasted, and I thought at the time that I should not mind if the 'regrading' committee — I felt compelled to put the word in inverted commas, it seemed so unreal and inappropriate — met a year hence instead of a few weeks.

The Colonel was a brisk, preoccupied man who would salute me on the stairs as we passed with a jovial, unvaried greeting, and not wait for me to hook any further additions on his remark, or make appropriate comments about the garden or the long hot summer, and I would mount the last flight with a sense of expectancy towards the day that stretched before me in that dusty, silent box-room with the cluttered brick-and-mortar street below that might so easily have been a wilderness of red and purple rhododendrons.

Then as I paused to switch on the electric-fan, I would

hear rising up the shaft of the stairs the clear, rounded voice of Mrs. Maybury, commenting on the morning's post or the front page of the paper, remarking on a cobweb on the ceiling, or pausing over a vase of dead flowers. And as I prepared to inscribe a number on to the spine of a book, or started separating geology from ecology in the vast section on natural history, her voice and her comments would float nearer and nearer till she was standing there in the doorway, small and smiling and weatherbeaten, in a broken straw hat, leaning half out, half in; half in sun, half in shadow, against the lintel, crying· 'Hallo, hallo, how punctually you turn out! All well? We must get you some fresh flowers in here, I think.'

'What a hot day!' she would sigh as she turned to go. 'How hot it is going to be again! I must get you some gladioli to take back with you; do you *like* gladioli, or would they be a nuisance *up there*? I'm glad to see the fan is working all right. Do you like all this heat?'

Usually I replied simply, 'Yes, I do,' and Mrs. Maybury would wander away murmuring:

'I must leave you in peace now, or Bertie will be on my tracks.' But it used to occur to me that the Indian jungle must be very much hotter than this, and once I ventured to add a little more and supplement our antiphon.

'I wonder whether the monkeys would be better off at the tops or the bottoms of the trees.'

We stood there thinking for a moment; one each side of the door, Mrs. Maybury clutching an empty vase, trying to decide, until she laughed and shook her head and said she did not know, and made her way down-stairs, clapping to the dog to come off her beds of basil, and calling to her husband not to forget her shopping list, and I returned to the pile of books: animal, vegetable and mineral.

She would return again later, with tea or coffee, and implore me to come outside for a 'breather' when I felt like it, or bring some work out to the canvas swinging couch or the summer-house and not to stay all day 'cooped up in that furnace'. I never accepted her offer though, because I was quite happy up there under the sweating roof looking down on the red-brick street broken up by the pickle-factory, the dancing academy and the long hoarding advertisement for 'ten o'clock tested beans'. Sometimes she would break off her dis-course about her son's forthcoming marriage, the best fertilizer for cinnerarias, or the articles of faith they ought to teach in prep-schools, and wrinkle up her fore-head, smile apologetically and sigh:

'I hope you are not feeling too lonely and solitary, my dear, all alone up here. I feel a bit guilty when I see you working away so industriously. I hope this is the right kind of place for you, and you are not feeling cut off and out of the swim.'

I wished I knew the right thing to say, the thing that would reassure her.

Instead of taking the bus back to the hospital at the end of the day, I would cross the park behind the May-

burys' street, and walk, between the black-cottonwood
trees that smelt of honey, and along the banks of a stream
until it was swallowed in an enormous pipe, and I come
out in the wide, paved avenue that led up the hill away
from the town. The road mounted slowly towards the
country, but before it reached the iron gates of Gardenwell Park on the summit, I discovered on one of my
leisurely tours that between two houses, 'Cranmere'
and 'St. Briavels', there was a green tunnel between
clipped hedges, and at the end, gleaming like an island,
the cool grey that was the hospital wall, solid and apart
from the fancy black-and-pink villas, the cement benches,
and smooth-tiled pavements that announced the beginning of the country. It was not hard to climb this wall,
and you dropped down easily into the soft, long grass
of the ha-ha on the other side. There was no pleasure
like this of dropping down from the road, and lying there
in a rough patch of land that had been overlooked by the
gardeners, and was full of poppies.

I seemed to spend most of my evenings there, lying in
the last of the sun with the birds flying round, leaning
against the wall that had suddenly swerved away from the
avenue of traffic and run off on its own among the fields.
I grew fond of this grey stone, and used to wonder why
visitors to the hospital grumbled because they had
crowned the hill with this monument, rather than with a
garden city.

The hospital was clearly a kind of settlement, I thought.
Perhaps they did not see this when they grumbled about

its size and its colour, and the high battlements that looked down over the city on one side and up to the hill on the other. It was a settlement, most certainly, and for the time when someone should ask me where I lived, I prepared a summary of what I imagined might be its story. What exactly it was dedicated to I was not quite sure. That was not clear, but it hardly mattered, for no one ever asked me where I lived. Mine was not the kind of life where you 'ran into old friends', or were 'looked up' by them. The Mayburys, of course, knew where I lived, but they made only embarrassed and half-closed references to those 'gentlemen up at the top of the hill', whom I began to picture like the royalty in a pack of playing cards.

So I would lie there for a long time in the evenings before returning to the ward, looking over beyond rough fields and tennis courts, to the hill, and invisible to the passers-by on the road or on the neat hospital walks. It was very rarely that anyone passed the ha-ha or strolled nearer to where I had settled myself among the flowers than the beech-walk that bordered the tennis courts. It was only once in those idyllic days of August that anyone came close enough to see me.

At first I thought it was a male nurse coming briskly over to tell me that the ha-ha belonged to the male nurses exclusively. But his mouth was not severe or pursed, and he looked at me only curiously with an expression that was half-smile, half-grimace.

Then I thought I recognized him. I thought he must be

the man I had often seen strolling up and down the drive
with a cigarette in his mouth and a book under his arm,
or stopping at the main doors to throw remarks to some
invisible person within.

He smiled and hesitated in his walk, and twisted on his
heel and sauntered across the poppies towards me. I felt
vaguely that he wanted something: wondered what it
could be.

'I must say,' he said when he was close enough, 'I feel
just like that too.' His face was pale, but his voice was
deep and firm and seemed to be full of amusement. I did
not quite see what he felt like, however.

'I beg your pardon?' I asked. 'Like what? What do
you feel like?' But he only sighed. He had fair hair that
clustered over his forehead, and large white teeth that
snapped out gleaming when he smiled, which was often.

'Been in this outfit long?' he asked, tapping at the
insides of his pockets.

'No, not very, at least not as long as some of them.'

'And have you solved the problem of killing time, or
have you resigned for the time being, as far as being
alive is concerned?'

'I never was bored,' I assured him. 'I've never been
bothered about how to pass the time. For one thing I
work during the day, at the Mayburys' in the town.
For another...'

'There does not look much wrong with you,' he
interrupted curiously.

'No, there isn't. I did have an illness, but that is past

now; that is ancient history, and I am just here till the committee meets next month. As a matter of fact, I have rather come to regard it as my home now that Mother is dead.'

'Sorry,' he said. 'Hard luck . . .' There was a pause. I noticed there was a little piece of *dendrex renata* suspended from his left ear. It looked as though it might fall at any moment.

'That must have been a blow. I'm very sorry,' he repeated.

'Don't mention it. It was an accident with the electric blanket. Simply an accident. Not that it wasn't a great blow.'

'I'm sure it must have been.'

There was another long pause.

'The trouble with this place is,' he began at last, sinking down into the long grass – I waited for the *dendrex renata* to fall from his ear on to his shoulder – 'it's just like the worst kind of private hotel. Television, tennis, clock golf, and five minutes to the town centre. And just the same types too. Soupy old boys, some of them. Oh dear,' he bent over and swung his head between his knees. 'Every day is identical with the one before. It's pathetic, grotesque. I literally can't tell them apart, except for Sunday which is too grey and musty to be confused with anything, even ashes and cold spinach. Sunday is always the worst. Primitive guilt, I suppose. A regressive festival! It would be a bit better if I could concentrate a little.' He threw his hands with a rush through his hair. 'But I can't even get through a 'tec. Whew!'

He shook his hair out between his knees again, and swung backwards and forwards.

'Excuse me,' I said, 'but if you do that I've lost my view.' You see the birds were wheeling into the sunset, behind the tower of the Liquifruta factory, towards the hill. I explained to him about the hill and how I one day meant to go beyond it.

'I see. Awfully sorry,' he apologized for spoiling my view, 'but sometimes it gets me that way. I long for someone to talk to, distraction, or a mild explosion. I want someone to hand out a few drinks. I long to see a few women! Oh dear. Such a lot of men all stuck together! We'll all end up as queers!'

He stopped abruptly and looked up at me. 'Pardon my curiosity, but why are you here? You look so ordi— so jolly healthy normal.'

'That's because I am supposed to be leaving soon. I shall be sorry though.' He pulled a face. 'I shall miss the place, especially climbing over the wall, and dropping down into the field at night.'

His eyes were wandering round. 'They are pulling that wall down, thank goodness,' he murmured. He seemed to be speaking more to himself than to me. 'At last someone's seen a glimmering of daylight in this antediluvian set-up. They've got the contractor already.'

'Why? Why should they do that?' I was puzzled.

'Well, I suppose someone's injected that truth into

them – namely that it makes the place look institutional; gives it a bad name. It's hardly likely that the idea just occurred naturally to them.'

'But it's part of the settlement,' I pointed out.

But he was not listening.

'I'm here because of tension. Nervous tension,' he was telling me. He laughed. He seemed to laugh a lot. His teeth flashed in and out. His hair bobbed up and down. 'Anxiety neurosis. On the ward they call it "me noives". Too many emotional crises in my life I suppose. I'm having analysis.' He put on a deep, thundering voice like Dr. Clements, 'Deep, profound searching, lasting, enduring analysis'.

'I'm sorry to hear it.'

'Thank you, not at all, don't mensh. It's obvious you are not here on account of too many emotional crises.'

'Emotional crises? It's a year since Mother died if that's what you mean.'

'No, I mean *crises d'amour*. Women,' he giggled, 'or rather men.'

'A man once kissed me, but it hurt. I think his teeth were rather too large or too protruding, or something.'

He giggled again. 'You cold pebble! Get thee to a nunnery! The trouble with me is that I lose my head each time, and let women down. I've let women down once too often.' The *dendrex* at last slipped from his shoulder back to its own. 'My performance is so poor.'

'Your performance?' I thought of amateur theatricals, but I did not want to interrupt him.

'My performance. So my G.P. stuck me in here for "profound, lasting and searching analysis", along with a lot of depressives and schizies.'

'Schizies. What are they?'

He was sitting upright, cross-legged and pulling up tufts of the grass. 'Oh, you know, schizophrenics, split personalities smitten with *la belle indifférence*. One of them talks about his messages and complains about the jam at breakfast in the same breath. Then there's the famous Miss Beauchamp case. A classic!'

'And the children I've seen playing at your windows, are they schizies?'

'David certainly is, but Jocelyn's epileptic.'

'And do they cure them, the schizies?'

'Not really. They prop them up a bit and make *some* improvement. They give them insulin and that does some good. But I got all this from the male nurse and "Meyer-Gros", so maybe it's not the last word. What treatment did you have by the way? Just pills and heart to hearts, or the high-jump?'

'I had insulin, but I daresay they give it for other things as well as what you said. I expect they do. I feel sure of that.'

'I'm sure they do.' He was sympathetic. 'I'm sure they do. But still it must have been very nasty.'

'I don't think about it. Mother used to say there were some things it was just not right to remember.'

'That's right. But what do you do with your day then? Aren't you laying about them for your discharge?'

I told him about the Mayburys and the classes I was sorting their books into, and the attic room with the view over the town. 'And in the evening I climb the wall and come in here, so it's simple.'

'But don't you ever get a bit tired of that? Don't you get fed up being shut up with a lot of nut cases? Don't you sometimes want to see real people?'

But I saw plenty of real people, I assured him. The Sister, for example, and the women in the street where I worked and the Mayburys.

'And you never want to go to a flick or out for a spin?'

'Mother and I sometimes used to go to the Saturday matinées at the Old Theatre. But when Mother died I rather dismissed them. In fact I began to brood rather and things began to get on top of me. That was why the Principal sent me here.'

'Poor old thing. I expect you were deeply attached to Moth— to your mother.'

'We were good friends. Only Mother used not to like the way I laughed so much. She used to call me "her giggly girl", or if it grew excessive, "the giggly one".' She would be surprised now, I thought, if she could see me doing a responsible library job and making decisions about the contents of the world.

'And why *did* you laugh so much?' he queried. 'I don't find it so very funny. It's positively gruesome sometimes – *la condition humaine*. Why did you laugh?'

'I don't know. Just that it seemed so funny being alive at all.'

'Funny! that was a rare gift. Did it all seem so funny, everything? And is that why the Principal sent you here? To cure you of your laughter?'

'Yes, I suppose that is why. But I must be going now as the Sister always comes in to say good night before she goes off duty.'

'Half a mo. Stay a few moments longer.' But I was already on my feet.

I had started off towards the beech-walk. 'Half a mo.' I stopped and turned. 'What a rare gift you had! What a pity to have to cure someone of their sense of humour! Why didn't you teach your mother and the Principal of your College to laugh too, instead of letting them send you here? Will you teach me to laugh sometime?' Then he stopped abruptly. 'Forgive my asking, but were you fond of your mother, or did you hate her?'

At the time I was very shocked. 'Of course I did not hate her. Mother and I were very "thick". We were very good friends,' I assured him as I went across the grass at a run.

Chapter Three

AFTER this, we would bump into each other quite often. We would meet in the recreation room at the Sunday evening record recitals, or he would wave to me from the benches beside the tennis courts. Or sometimes I would see him drifting across the grass towards the ha-ha, complaining of his boredom, the 'antediluvian techniques of this set-up', or the carryings-on of some town council in the paper that he was reading. Or sometimes when I was scaling the hospital wall on my return in the evening, he would be sitting by the ha-ha smoking and appraising my performance as I descended.

'How is it?' he would cry, stretching out his arms and yawning as I manœuvred for my descent. 'Slowly does it! Jump! How are you ticking over these days? How is the big bad world treating you? Jump!'

'It always treats me very well,' I would reply when I had jumped and come down beside him.

'I wish it did me,' he would grimace. 'I wish I knew the aim of this particular exercise,' and he would launch into an account of some incident that had happened on the ward that day, a piece of buffoonery on the part of one of the staff, or some set-back that he had received on his own account.

He said his name was Alasdair, Alasdair Faber, and that he had been a medical student at London when his *crise nerveuse* had started in earnest. He had realized that he could not carry on without taking some decisive step to help himself. It was then that he had 'downed tools' and retreated here, he explained.

He told me a lot about himself. He told me about his sailing, and how he had nearly been drowned off Pola in the Adriatic; he told me about the TR2 he was set on having when he was 'out of here'; he described to me the Italian and French films he had seen on the parole-days when he managed to escape to London; he tried to make me understand the character of 'Bergman', and he tried to make me understand his 'problem with women'.

I was puzzled; puzzled to know why he told me all this about women, as though I were not a woman; and puzzled to know why he went on bothering. 'But if they give you so much bother,' I objected one day, 'why *do* you bother?'

'*Sancta simplicitas*,' he smiled at me, 'I envy you your austere, uncomplicated life.' Then the whistle blew, and the 'long-stay' patients moved slowly past in their teams, shuffling their feet and dragging their spades behind them to the sheds, and Alasdair began to groan again about 'this outfit' and its methods.

'It was as though they had never heard of the nineteenth-century reforms, and all the new industrial techniques and forms of social therapy for the chronic... Does even that make you want to laugh?' he drawled with a mixture of sourness and amusement in his voice as the band of workers trailed past us to the sheds, and the male nurse blew a final sharp blast on his whistle. 'Do you never want to inquire what the aim of *that* particular exercise is? Do you *never* feel really indignant and angry?'

I thought hard, but I did not think so. 'It's a question of the way you look at things, I suppose.'

'Most things are,' he retorted dryly, twisting up the corners of his mouth.

He was lying on his face in the long grass, his chin dug into the ground, and I was sitting absently a little way off, examining some maiden-hair grasses. Music was coming from the recreation room. We could hear the social workers calling instructions for the 'Military Two-step' down the long room. We could hear their shouts, 'Come along Mr. Grey! Take a partner. Choose your man, ladies', and the disorganized, unrhythmic shuffling and bumping of many feet.

'Join in Gracie! Stir your stumps, Wilfred!' the orders came. 'Don't leave it all to the ladies.'

'That's called "rehabilitation", "resocializing",' Alasdair remarked sourly as the music started up again.

It was the band that they hired every week from the winter gardens, a saxophone, an accordion, and a lame drummer. 'It's like watching the *Titanic*,' he chuckled, 'with the band playing as the jolly old ship goes down. Still, I'd prefer to go down to the howls of the "Okey-Kokey" and the "Carolina Blues", than to "Nearer my God to Thee", wouldn't you?'

But I was thinking. I was trying to call up those feelings that he had just mentioned, indignation and anger.

'All those deteriorated men and women,' he went on, 'being pushed about to satisfy the sadistic instincts of the male nurses and social therapist, shouted at and wheeled about like children and having blue ribbons tied in their hair if they are female; and the breezy young doctors who fancy their duty has been done when they have inquired whether their patients prefer green or yellow or piebald jam at breakfast, and whether the rounders pitch is in good trim. It makes me puke. It makes me peel. God knows I'm not an "angry".' He rolled over on his back and stared at the sky. 'It's just a matter of common sense. Do you never want to rage at the whole bag? Does nothing *ever* rouse you?'

I was still trying to think.

I racked my brains, and tried hard to picture the feelings of anger and indignation. I tried to see the settlement as Alasdair saw it. I tried to picture the men working in a canning factory or sitting round the fire at ease, and feel anger that they were not. But something interfered between me and my potential wrath every time. It was just the picture of a town, the picture, perhaps, that I had from the Mayburys' top window, that prevented me from swellings of anger and indignation and the rest that Alasdair so well exemplified.

'The chanceyness of it all,' I tried to explain as he lay there blowing smoke out into the sky. The houses and the offices and the showrooms with the people going in and out. And the parks and patches of green in between the houses, all worn and sterile and punctured with the marks of sharp, narrow heels, pram-wheels and the stabs of umbrellas. Heels, umbrellas, pram-wheels, match-sticks and paper-bags with messages stamped on them. There were so many things in the world . . . and it might so easily not have been at all. It might so easily be rolled up and tossed aside into a bin, like a piece of paper and there be nothing there, just thick jungle. 'It is all too strange and chancey to be worried or angry about,' I finished. 'That's why. I might just as well try to be angry because I had found the wrong thing in a cracker at a Christmas dinner.'

But Alasdair was talking about something else, about social equality and the 'angries', and I do not even think he saw what I was referring to.

'Sorry,' he apologized, 'another of my *bêtes noires*. That garage I was telling you about,' he changed the subject, 'has promised to let me try out MXC 2937 tomorrow.'

The music had stopped. We fell silent, so silent that

you could hear the dry leaves and twigs creaking over the insects moving in the earth, and the boys kicking tin-cans on the waste patch, and the sounds of lawnmowers far away. It was like this often. The only other noise was Alasdair blowing smoke with sudden spurts of breath among the overshadowing trees, and giving little explosions, half sigh, half satisfaction, into the peaceful twilight.

'Good night, good night,' I would cry cheerfully as I made my way across the grass. He would raise his hand and wave me into the twilight 'So long.'

I never returned to the ward at night without meeting the Sister. She would put her head round the door crying:

'Am I welcome?' and settle herself on the end of the bed and we would talk.

I would tell her about my day at the Mayburys', or about my life with Mother at Wookens Walk, or the little cottage we used to rent at La Charrue every summer. She in her turn would talk about her life in Munich and the opera that she was so passionately fond of, or her escape to England, and her years in the intern-ment camp and among people whose language she did not speak.

'That was my small share of the wooden cross,' she would end, 'and you have had yours too.' Her voice would drop and she would abruptly thrust her hands under her apron, and leaning back against the iron frame of the bed murmur:

'Well dearie, and what about *you?*' and wait staring at
me.

It was as though she wanted me to confess some tragic
fact that she already knew about. 'How *is* it?' she would
press, as though she expected 'it' to be very bad instead of
very good. 'How goes the world? The big impersonal
world outside? Is there room in it for your personality,
and for your dreams? Or do we plunge you into it too
soon? Perhaps it was too early . . . ' She would trail
away thoughtfully, and sit there waiting, brooding at me
with her large, pensive eyes.

'No.' I used to have to reassure her. 'It isn't too soon.
I am very happy. It is . . . ' But I was stuck. I did not know
what would reassure her. 'It is good to be well again.'

'So! I am glad. But tell me,' she would insist, 'about
your *friends*. That I would like to see, that you should
fare well in your friendships.'

'There is a man called Alasdair on the male side,' I
said, hoping this would satisfy her. 'I sometimes bump
into him in the gardens and we sit there talking.'

'Yes? Really?' she remarked politely. 'That is good,
but I really meant a *real* friendship. A young woman of
your own age that you could go with to the cinema
sometimes, or in the country . . . what is it, to ramble . . .
at the week-ends. Someone from your own culture and
milieu. A friend, that I would like to see.' She rolled her
'r's dramatically. 'A soul-friend.'

Her dark eyes would fill with earnest thought, but she
would only pause, then say 'good night dearie' and

disappear. When she had gone there was always a German chocolate or a heart-shaped gingerbread propped on the mantelpiece or hidden behind the photograph of Mother on the window-sill. I ate it guiltily. I knew there was something that was the right thing to have said, something that would reassure her that I had made the grade and had 'come through', only I did not know what it was.

It was almost as difficult at the Colonel's house. My attic was like the top branches of a tree, and I would stare down entranced at the world below. But as I watched, Mrs. Maybury would appear with coffee.

'When you find it a bit too quiet, up here all on your own,' she would smile, 'do come down into the garden for a bit of sun. I do hope you are liking us...' She would raise her voice, waiting like the Sister for me to corroborate something. But I could never find, however hard I struggled with words, the thing she expected.

There was the widow in the house opposite, tending a sick parrot, and finding flowers left on her doorstep by a kind neighbour; there was the baby lying on the bed in the flat above; the mentally defective boy crouched on the wall, hiding his face from the sun or boasting to the younger children who crowded laughing round him. A gentle wind was blowing the curtain out. The door hovered backwards and forwards with a tiny creak. The sky suddenly was still. I wanted to point to that; just to that scene and cry:

'Look, look, that is my answer to your remark. Look

at the street, the sky. How still it is all of a sudden! Everything is suspended! It is the perfect moment.'

There she was, still standing and smiling with her hair waving slightly in the draught. A silence stretched all round us as though everything had stopped to catch this moment. I smiled at her in satisfaction. I nodded. I was almost gloating. Her usual smile increased to a beam.

'Soon my daughter will be coming to stay with her children,' she said. 'Then perhaps it will be a bit more lively for you. Do you like children?'

The moment was lost and things began to move on again.

'I am so glad you are liking us,' she was saying. 'I hope you will want to stay it out until our little library is finished. Soon I suppose they will be giving you a clean bill of health, the gentlemen up at the hospital, and you will be wanting to take off! You'll be wanting to launch out into something better with a proper salary and a more exciting atmosphere where you will be meeting other people. That will be a great pity for us.' She laughed. 'When Bertie and I first met . . . ' she laughed again. 'We hardly knew we were young . . . '

Just then the postman rattled below and she excused herself and went down and I saw what she meant by 'launching out'. They thought I and my life ought to be different. But I was anxious. I wanted to be clear, so I ran after her. She was still standing by the front door talking to the postman when I caught her.

'You mean. Did you mean that my life ought to be different?' I began.

'My dear, I only meant that we like having you here, and, she paused, 'youth is short, you know, and if ever you want to push off early because of a party or anything, don't hesitate to say so.'

So I left the Mayburys' early that day. Not because of a party or anything, but because I wanted to be back at the order. I started walking swiftly towards the park. I wanted to be sitting in the ha-ha alone. But at the end of the Mayburys' street something happened to stop me. It was hot, and someone was calling at me. 'Yooeee, yooeee.' I looked round but I could not see anyone. 'Yooeee.'

I was surprised. I had never been arrested like this before. I had never before been called upon like this to stop what I was prosecuting. But someone was certainly hailing me from across the street, and asking me to stop still where I was. I knew that I ought to do so, and look up and see and recognize the person who was calling out at me from the lowered window of a little grey car.

'Hallo.' She leaned out, calling softly and huskily with a slight lisp that seemed familiar. She wore a tangerine-coloured dress, and her hair was coiled up smoothly under a hat that was like a snowflake. She smiled faintly.

'Hallo,' she called. Her voice was cool and clear, but distant, spreading slowly out over the hot summer afternoon. 'I did not think you were ever going to deign to notice me,' she almost whispered.

Her smile widened. She stretched over to the other seat, and I saw that it was Helena, Helena Bruce, an old college friend whom I had not seen since I left Somerville. That was over a year ago.

'It seems ages.' She was grinning now and leaning over, and pressing on the door of the car. She was fiddling with the catch to open it, I saw, but I seemed wedged against it, staring down at her sunburnt face, the dark interior of the car, and the little personal objects that she had scattered among the shiny pieces of apparatus.

'How are you?' She stared at me with her dark brown eyes. 'Where have you been hiding yourself since you disappeared off the scene last year, just before "schools"? We all thought you were set for a "first" and a fellowship, but when you were suddenly swallowed up in darkness and no one knew your whereabouts,' the faint, cool smile reappeared on her lips, 'we all supposed you had beetled off to darkest Africa as you always threatened.'

There was a pause. She had given up trying to open the door, and she simply leaned on the window-sill with her chin tilted up to the sun. 'Was the lure of Africa not so strong after all? And how's the *Ormulum*?'

'I never got to Africa,' I croaked harshly. I felt oddly big and clumsy and padded beside her. 'I've had to change my plans. In fact a lot of things have changed since those days.'

She raised her eyebrows for a moment, and then dropped them.

'For better or for worse?' she murmured absently. She was staring up and down the grey street. 'Do you work here or something? We all thought you would dig yourself in at Oxford.'

She smiled and drew herself a little closer. A vague pleasant smell of scent and new leather came up at me. I saw her fingers in rows, all separate, clasping at the lowered window of the car. Her voice softened and lowered.

'My life's changed a lot too,' she said shyly, and started to tell me how she had planned to do a 'management course' when she went down, 'but since then,' she laughed a little, she had 'thrown it up. For one thing, the set-up was far too hierarchical, and anyhow,' she grimaced and shaded her face, she did not really think she 'ever wanted to go far in the chocolate-making line. Partly . . .' she hesitated and shrugged.

There was a pause. She looked mysteriously into the heat. I seemed to be causing some confusion with a couple of vans on the street. There was some swerving and hooting.

'Come round the other side,' she stretched over and pushed the door open, 'and then we can talk . . . As I was saying,' she continued as I pressed myself into the driver's seat, 'partly because after Oxford, chocolate hardly seems a career, and anyway, I doubt if I want a career now . . . I'm so involved with Tony.'

Marriage had caught up on her, she explained after some hesitation and a little wry smile that made me think I ought to condole.

'I'm very sorry...' I began.

'Take my advice,' she interrupted, with a little burst of mirth. 'Don't let yourself get caught up in it. It's such a bore! Be wise and stay outside the game like a sensible intellectual.'

I was staring out of the driver's seat, taking in every word she said. She looked me up and down.

'But how are *you*? I've talked a lot about myself.'

But I did not know how to talk about myself. I did not know how to tell her about the settlement or the ha-ha or the view from the Mayburys' attic window. I just stared at the tiny pair of shoes that she had abandoned beside the gear handle, and the chain of keys that she fingered thoughtfully.

'How I miss those days!' she went on. 'I still have pangs for college life and those long evening discussions that we used to have.' She grinned, faintly embarrassed. 'And when you go down, you fall back into all the old conformist patterns of behaviour.' She told me about her engagement, and all the wedding preparations. 'It's all a terrible bore!' she sighed, 'terribly peripheral compared with Oxford. Sickening. Daddy has given me this Morris Minor. Isn't she a sweetie? Her name's the Rabbitt.'

We sat there and talked, at least Helena talked. She gave me news about our mutual college acquaintances. She told me about Tony Houghton, to whom she had got

engaged. She told me about their plans for when they
were married. 'I'm going to go on working of course.
Tony says he would hate a wife who was just a vegetable . . . But what about you?' she started fumbling
with her gloves. 'What did you say you were doing?
And where are you hanging out?'

I thought of the settlement. I remembered the descrip-
tion I had drawn up for this very occasion, but sitting
there in the driver's seat with Helena beside me cool and
poised and unfolding plans, I saw it had failed me. I
scrambled out of the car, almost falling with my face
against the pavement, and she slid back into her own
seat:

'Just there,' I whispered thickly, pointing. 'Down there
on the right. Twelve William Street. It's a catalogue I'm
doing.'

'A catalogue? That sounds very cerebral. What of?'

'Oh everything. Everything there is.'

She grimaced and took down 'Twelve William Street'
in a minute red leather book that had her initial in the
corner.

'Do come round some time,' she was saying, 'I'm
staying here with my aunt.' She scribbled her phone
number; her bag snapped to; she drew on her gloves.
'Tony's home's here you see, so I'm having the full dose
of the family. Did you see about Prue's engagement as
well? Sally, by the way, is in her father's business. She's
got her teeth into poor John's neck feathers. But do come
round some time and talk about old times and,' she

giggled slightly, 'set the world to rights again. You make me feel nostalgic, and Tony would love to meet you again, and some of our year have promised to come up some time to a small kind of engagement party.'

Helena's smile widened and she let in the clutch. 'So, now that we are neighbours, we must make up for lost time. Do look us up! Don't forget! I'm stagnating horribly away from Oxford and things intellectual.'

A thin tissue of paper with a telephone number scrawled on it blew at me in a draught of hot air. The car started up.

'Look the other way please,' Helena laughed, 'as I take this corner. The instructor would have a fit if he saw me. Don't forget,' she leaned out and called back at me, 'you've got the number. Any time. I'm literally vegetating in this town. Tony says I'm almost a cabbage already. So much for the higher education of women.' But she looked pleased and happy in spite of the apparent failure of the higher education of women.

The car slid off down the road leaving me with a wisp of soft paper, and a faint, sweet smell of scent and cloth and new warm leather. I jerked down the road and across the park, pursued by Helena's clear, floating voice, her smile, and her snowflake hat. I suddenly thought of Sally and Prudence too, and their well-articulated voices above those of the men, laughing and talking across noisy, smoke-filled rooms as I made my way home from the Camera in the evenings.

They came back to me clearly. I realized that I had not

forgotten anything; not Helena's world, the complete
and certain world of men and women; not those nights
when I would pass underneath the lighted windows of
colleges and the big houses in North Oxford where the
laughter rose higher and louder as the hour grew later.
I had not forgotten those parties; I used to catch a
glimpse of them when the curtains were not drawn –
the talk, the arguments, the clink of glasses, the shadow
of bare arms, and smooth sculptured heads. And behind
them all, the flicker of candlelight against the wall and the
soft, crying voices of the jazz quartet like people who had
been locked up, breaking out in tears and laughter.

It was all still printed clearly on my mind, only when
it came back, it was with a pang. It had all seemed so
remote and unreal then. I used to stop and stare in awe
for a moment as I passed. I used to take in with amaze-
ment this poised, confident world of men and women
who never seemed to have any doubts about existence. I
would stand in there my sensible shoes that would 'fill
the bill on most occasions', and the plain wool dress that
Mother and I had bought together on one of our well-
thought-out expeditions up to 'the big West End stores'.

And there was Mother, small and neat with her wispy
hair flying, beaming good-humouredly at the assistant
as she paid the bill, crying: 'Well, we have had a good
innings this morning!' as we made our way to our
home-base, clutching our purchases. 'Good enough for
our little budget at any rate.' For Mother belonged to the
old school who would not accept grants from local

authorities – 'Or rather,' she would say with her wry
little smile, 'money from the taxpayer's pocket' – for her
daughter's education.

There she was, above the whirr of the coffee-grinder
in the grocer's shop explaining to Mr. and Mrs. Patrix-
bourne, our good neighbours, why I ran through them
all rather quickly at the University, and why life for me
was not a 'gay whirl of social activity'. Had the laughter
receded only to leave me high-and-dry staring through
those windows, never wanting to go inside? Or would
the window be flung open, and someone call me in?
When the invitation arrived about a fortnight after my
meeting with Helena at the corner of William Street, I
did not know.

At first I just stared at the invitation, and put it back in
its envelope slowly, numbly and awkwardly. This must
be what Mrs. Maybury had meant by being in the swim
and leaving my work early sometimes for parties and
things. I supposed too that this was what the Sister had
meant by getting back into the outside world and finding
my place among real people. I felt vaguely that after all
this must be what life was about. Arms and legs and
eyes ... it was easy to see their purpose. But life ... we
did not know what *that* was for. Perhaps the candlelit
world of parties and people was a way of feeling one's
way into the real world.

And yet I was not sure. So I just stared at the invitation
that Mrs. Maybury had perched on the edge of the basket

chair as though it were a strange thing: the small, unfamiliar white envelope addressed 'Miss Josephine Traughton, 12 William St., Wolverton'. And inside something stiff and square which summoned me to a party, a cocktail party, given by Miss Helena Bruce and Mr. Tony Houghton, at 3 Waterminster Place.

I just fumbled and stared. Even the names moved me. 'Miss Helena Bruce'; 'Miss Josephine Traughton': strange collocutions that just happened to refer to us, and there might so easily have been some mistake. When I thought of all the Josephines there must be in the world, and also the moderate numbers of Traughtons, it occurred to me that it might so easily have been just by a slip or a coincidence that in the hurly-burly and the paperwork of life the invitation had happened to fall on me, just as it had happened to fall on the shoulder of the basket chair in the room where I worked.

For I was not the kind of person that was invited to parties, I told myself, any more than men kissed me or I ran into old friends in the street. But I *had* run into old friends... just that.

But, my objecting self went on, just as men told me about their women friends, women would tell me about their parties and the dresses with zips all the way down the back that sometimes got stuck at five or six in the morning when you were longing to be in bed. This I knew was one of the bores of life, as were the men who did not wear gloves when they danced and clasped your bare back with their 'great sweating paws'. Great bores, great bores, I was made to understand, and I was sure it must be true. But it had never had anything much to do with me.

Yet here it was, the invitation. I stared at the card in hesitation and doubt. 'Miss Josephine Traughton'. It was the hit-or-miss of these words that struck me most. I knew the collocution was supposed to represent me and no one else, but it always seemed odd that so loose an approximation as a name could have a claim on you, could intervene in your life, could summon you to the gallows, or to a party out of the blue like that.

There was also another thing that made me hesitate and fumble with the invitation. As I have said, I was not very often invited to parties at Oxford. Only one invitation in fact had ever come my way, and that was the time that Mother had died. Had not the Sister instructed me to look at the future, not at the past? So I pushed aside the invitation. After all, there were at least twenty-two Traughtons in the London-area telephone book alone. The card might so easily have been for one of the others . . .

And yet the protests faded out and I was left with the memory of that other invitation that had come just a few days before Mother had died and I came to Gardenwell Park; the stiff white card announcing my name and hers in such a pre-established way, inviting me to Miss Veronica Piercy's—she who had protested about the Aldermaston Marchers—for drinks at Lennox Gardens just before the beginning of the next term.

We were sitting at breakfast when it arrived; at least
we had just finished. Mother was folding up the *Telegraph*
with her businesslike smile and (as was our usual plan of
campaign in the mornings) was scraping the marmalade
spoon and arranging the crockery on the trolley while I
fetched out my books.

There was the *Dream of the Rood* and the commentary
on the *Ormulum*, and there hidden underneath was an
Outline of Biology that I had bought in order to acquire
some understanding of the animals. I thought it might help
me to go abroad when I had graduated and gain a first-
hand knowledge of living things in some tropical country
where civilization had not yet affected them. I had already
begun to look through the papers for advertisements and
things, and I had borrowed a *Manual of Seamanship*
which might come in handy on the journey over.

Mother had left the trolley when she heard the postman's click, and she was standing there laying the
envelope before me, waiting with a quiet hovering little
pause as I opened it. I could hear her breathing and the
muted creakings of her stomach as she stood there.

I drew out the card. A party. Drinks. A pause.

'May we ask about it?' she asked at length in her bright,
interested way, standing by my shoulder. 'Unless, of
course, it's a "top secret",' she added musingly with her
head on one side, her eyes glinting mischievously.

'A friend. A college friend,' I told her. Miss Piercy
had once invited me to the Chaplaincy.

'You looked browned off, Miss Traughton,' she had

called across to me in the common-room one day as I was staring at some catmint. 'May I help?' She told me her name was Veronica but she preferred to be called 'Perry'. 'May I help?' she had asked.

I had assured her that it was nothing but that I always did get slightly bothered about the nature of reality. At this she brightened and agreed that she used to get frightfully bothered too at one time, and explained that she thought my trouble might be the same as hers, namely, non-alignment.

She sat down on the window-seat beside me and suggested that if I could bring myself round to accepting the painful (almost agonizing, if we could really see) fact of the Incarnation, I could understand how God can see us down here in all our mess and misery.

She also told me about Alec at the Chaplaincy who could be frightfully clear and helpful when you were 'all bogged up and could not get into gear and take-off and all that'.

Mother was waiting with her inquiring little smile. I knew she disliked discourteous and cavalier responses, so I was none too happy.

'What are their names, my dear?' she was repeating, looking over her glasses warmly. 'It is usual to let older and wiser, at least, more experienced, heads' – she gave her dry little chuckle – 'look over an invitation, my dear. Just to give it the glance over.'

So I handed the card over to Mother, and after a pause

she tapped me playfully on the shoulder with it, and remarked (I could see she was pleased):

'I see my daughter is blossoming out. I see my Josephine is branching out on her own and breaking new ground. She'll be a high-flyer yet.'

Mother returned to the trolley, but in a moment she was back, tapping me this time with her rolled-up napkin:

'I shall soon be having a real all-rounder for a daughter,' she said with a meaningful glint. 'I have a feeling that you will soon be meeting your match in the world, and I shall be seeing less of you!'

I was afraid she might have guessed about the *Manual of Seamanship*, and put two and two together, but she went on:

'Youth is still something that is not to be had for the buying, and young men, I know, are cavalier and out for the main chance. We shall have to sit down sometime and put our heads together and think about ways and means, if you are to fill the bill. We must think about clothes and times of last buses back from Lennox Gardens to the "home base".'

Mother quoted the parable of the man who came to the wedding without his wedding garment and was turned away, and we decided there and then that on Saturday, two days before the party (and a well-deserved little Sabbath after the moil of book-work), I would launch myself on the West End and buy a really smart dress, one that would really fill the bill.

Mother suggested coming with me. She seemed a little anxious lest wily assistants should coax me into buying the wrong kind of dress, one that I should not feel very much at home in afterwards at Wookens Walk.

'There are plenty of people ready to tempt us out of our own particular little groupings, but with the two of us sticking together, we shall be proof against the wiliest shop-girls.'

I do not like to confess this, but I put Mother off. Partly because we lived a long way 'out', and the journey up to the West End might be rather trying for Mother who was not so young as she used to be. Partly because it was too difficult to explain why I wanted a certain kind of dress, not a quiet wool one that would do for Christmas and when the cousins came to the house.

Mother seemed to understand and simply said:

'I know when it is time for those older ones among us to step back and let the younger generation have a chance to blossom out.'

She folded her hands, put her head on one side and gave her mischievous little smile. I think she was rather pleased with me and the way I was coming out of my shell. I do not think I had giggled now for several months.

'When do you propose to launch off on your jaunt?' she asked as she crept in at eleven with our mid-morning drink. There was a glint in her eye as she tapped the Nescafé spoon and replaced the lid. She started bustling round, pretending to be busy and concerned only with household affairs, but we soon had our heads together bending over the table and mapping out my itinerary, Mother really entering into the spirit of it.

We had worked out how long it would take to get up to the Big Stores, which was the best way to get there (not necessarily the quickest way, but the all-round best, taking into consideration public buildings and monuments, junctions, fellow-passengers, and their sundry walks of life).

We had just started discussing where I should take up the assault on the fine shops when the disturbing thing happened.

'The early bird gathers the worm,' Mother was saying, and it would be best, if I was to cut new ground, to set out rather early. Then I should be flying out with my worm before all the crowds got going.

We were washing up our few crocks from the mid-morning drink, and we were laughing rather at the idea of my gallivanting off alone to help myself, so to speak, to the West End. We were wondering what the neighbours would think, for Mother had explained to them so often that I had no time for 'small-measure, light-weight things'.

As I said, we were washing up our few things, and Mother was tipping the water out of the bowl. But alas, it did not run away. It just stood there resting. Mother gave a vexed little cough and bent down and peered into the engineering work of the sink. Then she gave another little click of consternation, and poked with a skewer, and shook her head, and said after a little exploration:

'A blockage,' and how she wished there were a man about the house.

She bent down underneath the sink with a spanner and fumbled till water came rushing out into the bowl that she had thoughtfully provided. Then she shook her head and said we had better go and investigate outside, and make sure that nothing was blocked at the exterior end of the drain.

We went outside, and there Mother located the source of the trouble. The drain was choked; indeed it was stuffed. There was a pad of rotten dead leaves, a scum of coffee grounds, a few hairs, a bubble of soap detergent, and heaving up and down on top of them all was a snail. It was naked. It had no shell. It just lay there flapping to and fro.

Mother stood there, face to face with it for a moment, and then she drew in her lips as though she were at the battle-line. The look of consternation spread over her face.

It was rather odd to see them there face to face, and neither making the first move, at least, neither making the first *act*, for the snail was moving, though not progressively, the whole time.

Then Mother picked up a little piece of stick and, making slight reproachful noises in her throat, she thrust it at the pad, and while she made these feeble advances on the snail, her hair flew up and her glasses shone, and I could see behind her the washing-line, the rows of nylon underclothes, the coloured plastic pegs and the basket to cradle them in. And while the snail beat up and down, the neighbour's wireless played. I carefully suppressed a smile at these two opposite ends of existence coming together like that.

'Josephine, my dear,' Mother was calling rather sharply. She was panting slightly with the exertion of trying to lift the grid. I wondered if the snail were panting too. 'Just slip upstairs and fetch me my other glasses from the bedside table.'

I went up obediently. The bedroom was still rather stuffy with the smell of bedding and sleep. I sat down beside the small table and noted the owl-lamp that sent out a gentle beam when you touched a knob, the tin of biscuits for when Mother slept poorly, the Bible, and the Union reading leaflets. You read a portion of these every night. I thought of the snail flapping defiantly downstairs, and my eyes went back to the bed.

'The foxes have holes,' I thought, 'and the birds have their nests, but the son of man . . .' This suddenly seemed to be wrong. Looking at Mother's bed, I saw it must be the other way round, and I wished I could remember what 'Perry' and Alec had said about the animal kingdom, or whether they had said anything at all.

I stared again at the bed, and the wires and plugs of the electric blanket running out of the mattress, the tin of biscuits, and the Bible Union leaflets. I thought of Mother reading her nightly portion, 'stoking up' as she would say, digesting a biscuit, or lying, grey and withered, with Father, while round her raced the arthropods, the pigs, the hippopotami, the even-toed ungulates and the ruminants (rumini?). They pranced and they danced, and I laughed and laughed. I had not laughed so loudly, so coarsely, since the Principal's tea-party. Mother came rushing up, flushed and anxious.

'Josephine, my dear, Josephine,' she looked severe, but sad too. 'Try to pull yourself together, I have not seen the giggly one for such a long time! What has happened to all our good resolutions?'

I tried to control myself. 'Mother,' I began, pressing in my lips, 'about the snail in the drain, I hope all is well in that direction? I hope that little matter has been cleared up satisfactorily?'

But I was still choking, while the animals romped round the bedside table, and round Mother who was grey and withered.

'Try to keep off slugs and spiders and sundry things like that,' she said sharply. 'We don't make cant about things like that. It is just a not very interesting part of nature's economy, to keep things balanced.' Then she went on more quietly:

'You know we are all in the scheme of things, my dear. Sleepy caterpillars and spiders that make you feel creepy, and monkeys that are supposed to be intelligent – but you must remember that their intelligence is not creative or constructive. It is all directed to the satisfaction of animal needs, and they have no idealisms as we humans have. There is the ladder, you remember, and at the top is man, but quite different. In a sphere of his own. You must remember this from the book we used to read together when you were little.'

Her voice grew more and more distant. My mind wandered away. I wondered how she would fare among the cephalopods or the artiodactyles. They had such a lot in common, but they were so different.

'What is troubling you, my dear?' Mother's voice was pursuing, miles away. 'If it is about the party, we could easily ring up your nice friends and tell them things are not kindly disposed to us at the moment. Or if it is the dress . . . we could easily slip round to the Miss Wellses, and have some renovations done on your pretty green...'

But it was neither of these.

We just stood silent by the empty bed where Mother had lain with Father . . .

'For instance,' I said at length, 'for instance, suppose there were six leopards and six ladies, would you, *ought you*, to say, "twelve legs human and twenty-four legs leopard", or should one rather say, quite straight and simply, "thirty-six legs and six tails"?'

At length Mother repeated in a small, tired voice, 'We don't, *you know* we don't, make bones about things like that.'

Nevertheless it was a question.

She looked sad and pale, but at that stage of my

laughter, neither her reproaches nor her sadness could check me. It was existence itself that I was laughing at.

I went up, as we had planned, to the West End stores, and I even bought a straight, sheath-dress. But I never wore it, because it was that night that Mother had the accident with the electric blanket. It was as though my laughter had killed her. So you see, there was another reason why I was so doubtful about Helena Bruce's invitation.

I thought about it for several days, and finally one evening when I saw Alasdair playing tennis with the receptionist who sat at the *guichet* at the main door, I took the card out to him for his inspection.

He waved to me and smiled and went on with his game, so I sat down on the tarmac at the edge of the court till he had finished and came striding over, hot and panting, and flopped down beside me waving good-bye to his friend.

'How's life, Josephine?' he panted. 'How's way out beyond? What's this, well, what's the trouble?' as I held out the card, faltering:

'I suppose it's really meant for me, only I don't know whether I should go or not; whether it's not all a big misunderstanding.'

He lowered himself, flushed and still breathing heavily, on to his elbow and pulled at the card. It was several days since I had seen him to speak to. He had not been near the ha-ha, and I had assumed that his 'deep, profound searching and lasting analysis' was over, and that he must be gone.

'Let's have a dekko.' He pushed aside his racket and examined the card. 'Well, what's the trouble?'

'Well, what's the difficulty?' he repeated, slowly dragging his sweater over him, 'Helena Bruce and Tony Something are seeking you out, or rather they were only it's too late. Oh no, beg your pardon, it's tomorrow, the sixteenth. Well, look pleased. Smile. *Souriez Gibbs!* It's time someone enticed you back from your underworld isn't it? How old are you?'

'Twenty-three.'

'Well then,' he leaned back against the netting and looked at me thoughtfully. For the first time he did not seem to be laughing or sneering at something. His face was authoritative and thoughtful. 'It's about time you started casting your net out a bit wider isn't it? You can't keep up this exile for ever. Most people are thinking seriously about husbands at your age. So it's about time you got back into circulation isn't it? After all, you can't spend your whole life here sitting against that wall, and soon, I suppose, they'll be wanting to give you the push from here. You must rehabilitate yourself, as they would say.' He fidgeted and started to get up to go.

I suppose he was right. He was giving me advice. He was pushing me on into the future where I had been content to lie and wait for eternity. But I hesitated.

'It puzzles me . . . that of all the people they could have invited, they happened to have picked on *me*. I just wonder whether they could have really meant it, especially as I was never in the swim, so to speak, at Oxford. I never went to parties except committee teas of the Anglo-Saxon Society and bun-fights of the Christian Union and ...'

'I know the kind,' he guffawed. 'Quiet little gatherings of people of good will. Was there a prayer of recollection at the end? I know the kind,' he chuckled. 'Isn't that all the more reason for making a radical break with your past?'

'Yes, but I don't think I should be very good at the other kind of party.'

'The other kind?'

'The men and women kind. For one thing, I should not know what to wear ... unless of course it's fancy dress?' I added hopefully.

'Hardly likely.'

He studied my tweed box-pleat skirt and green corduroy jacket. 'Do you always adopt such a male attitude towards clothes?'

'There was never any real sympathy between us,' I confessed, 'except for the green jacket which I always think is like a field of ripening oats, and when I am feeling optimistic it is full and green and waving, and when I am "down", the field is low and flat and dead — otherwise I never really bother overmuch. Clothes always seem as though they are just pinned there, waiting to fall away. Not really mine at all, whatever I wear. Contingent, if you see what I mean.'

He roared with laughter, and sat down again. 'Have a heart on the poor chap, whoever he is.'

'Oh it isn't a man. It's Helena who has invited me to the party, an old college friend, at least an acquaintance. I used to know her because she had the next-door room to mine, and I used to help her with her Anglo-Saxon. She sometimes used to drop in late at night for some help, when she had said good-bye to her friends, and we would have a drink and sometimes some long discussions, and jokes too.'

'Well, bring me back some of the jokes then, not too blue though, as I am supposed to be *en vacances* from all that. I hope you have a good time.'

'You think I should accept then?'

'I can only repeat that it's about time you made a break with your past before they sling you out on your neck. I wish it were me invited to a party. I'd like to be going to a really good one tonight with plenty to drink and some new records and a splendid euphoria all round.'

But I was still in doubt. 'I should not know what to say, what to talk about.' As I have said, I always had some difficulty in knowing how the replies fitted on.

He laughed, rather sharply, it seemed. 'You don't seem to be having much difficulty now,' and began examining a bruise on his leg.

'I should be at a loss . . .' I began, but he interrupted impatiently: 'Don't start all that again. Surely that's all over now, that happened a long time ago and you were ill

then. Well, smile! Say cheese! You can look quite
pretty when you smile.'

I felt myself sweating. I could feel it emerging on my
upper lip as he rubbed his bruise and fiddled with his
racket and put it back into its frame.

'Oh surely not,' I protested uneasily. 'I don't think
you are quite right there. Mother used to say,' I was
shaking slightly, 'that though the content was good, the
vessel was an ordinary, workaday affair . . . A man on a
galloping horse would not stop.'

'Some criterion that, the galloping horse one!' He
stopped and stared at me. 'Don't you hate your Mother?'

The sweat was on my forehead now. I thought of the
lighted rooms and the voices, and I was always outside.
'I got used to her,' I hedged.

'Aren't you glad she's dead?' he persisted relentlessly.
There was silence. There was his clear, relentless face
searching me. I could hear the modern jazz quartet, and
the laughter from the college rooms. 'You are free now,'
he seemed to be saying. I wanted to run away from him.
'You are free now,' something shouted at me, remorse-
lessly. It seemed like my conscience saying that, and I
blurted out with vehemence at last. 'I am glad! I'm glad
she's dead. The future can begin.'

He smiled at me in a new way, I thought.

'Tomorrow to fresh fields and pastures new,' he
murmured. 'Twenty-three! Time you were looking for a
husband. The sixteenth, that's tomorrow. You'd better
reply *tout de suite*, or you'll miss the post.'

He held out the invitation card for me to take. 'Here, you'll be wanting this to reply.' He held it between his thumb and finger, waving it up and down. But I did not take it. His thumb and fingers were very small and round, with pale nails like pools of water. I stared at them.

'Here,' he said again. But I still did not take it.

'You are sure it is all right then?' I delayed.

'I expect so.' He still held it there.

I leaned over and opened my mouth and bit the corner of the card and snatched it from him with my teeth. For a moment he looked surprised, then he smiled approvingly.

'That's right, that's the spirit.' But I was choking with laughter. It came suddenly in a great guffaw and did not seem to be mine. I was shaking with nervousness.

'You've got a laugh like a disused lavatory cistern,' he remarked nonchalantly, pushing himself on to his feet and brushing the small pebbles from his legs.

'That's because you are right; things have changed. Of course I shall go to the party.' I longed suddenly to be there. I saw myself entering the long, candlelighted room with the jazz gently sighing and crying. 'I will slip silently and secretly into the real world as though I had never been absent,' I cried. 'What shall I wear? What does one wear on an occasion like this?'

'Wear what you like,' he was half-way from me, 'only don't laugh like that at Helena Bruce's or the big bad world will spit you swiftly back into this particular outfit. Enjoy yourself!' He was half-way across the court. 'Smile nicely, and flash your eyes at them, and if they don't make advances on you, you must make up the quota yourself.'

I was laughing again with pleasure and surprise. It came like water gushing uncontrollably out of a burst pipe. Then I remembered what Alasdair had said about the lavatory pan and stopped.

It was too late to reply to the invitation I decided, but for the first time since I had been here in my new quarters at the settlement I went to my locker on the landing and pulled out the contents and examined them. There were a few books, a Swahili grammar, a map of the Thames and Severn Canal, some shells, a few plant bulbs and a bundle of clothes.

There was the straight sheath dress I had bought without Mother. I pushed it aside vehemently. I wanted to forget it. I shook out a grey flannel skirt. It was crumpled and shiny, and there was nothing to go with it except a pink jumper that an old man had knitted for me in the occupational therapy hut. Besides being too short in the sleeve, it was strained and knotted where he had skipped stitches in his anxiety to be taken back to Balichery. I remembered how he had pounced out of the laurel bushes and handed it to me, saying in triumph that he was going back to Balichery next week. But I also remember seeing him a month later wandering blankly round the airing court with a white bandage cap on his head.

I lay on my bed with the contents of the locker heaped round me. The old man's moods of misery and nostalgia

were written all over the uneven stocking stitch of the
jumper, and I wished I had a new dress. I thought of the
women in pictures whose dresses seemed to belong to
them and grow from them like petals from a flower,
and I wished vaguely that the party were to be fancy
dress. There was that scene in *Le Grand Meaulnes* where
Augustin reappeared from the *terrain inconnu* wearing
under his jacket the *gilet de soie*. A silken waistcoat,
le gilet de soie, I thought drowsily, as I lay there half
asleep, half dreaming of the *terrain inconnu*.

The supper gong disturbed my reverie, and the smell
of baked beans on toast floating along from the dining-
room. I went down to supper dazed and happy and
hungry for the party, my first party. 'I will swim back
silently,' I thought, 'as though I had never been absent.'

Chapter Four

I TOOK GREAT delight in announcing casually to Mrs. Maybury that if it were convenient I should like to leave William Street a little early that evening on account of a very important engagement. I stood in the door of their dining-room – they were just finishing lunch – and told them about the party. The Colonel smiled at me as he peeled an orange; a look of satisfaction came over Mrs. Maybury's face, and we went into the garden together – this was the first time I had been into their garden – and wandered between the rose-bushes looking for the right rose to go with my jumper.

'I am so glad,' Mrs. Maybury had murmured, beaming as she straightened the *Ascolaria*. 'I am so glad,' she said dreamily. 'I hope it's a good party.' She bent forward and stretched among the roses and drew at one.

'How about him? If it's a silk, "cashmerey" kind of sleeveless affair, that just cries out for this almost-coffee

colour with that rough, leathery green leaf.' She put it
against me. 'Take any that you feel like, my dear.'

She had wandered off in search of her straw sun hat,
and I had sat down among the lavender-beds and
watched the bees floating to a hole in the wall, while the
heat came over the garden in waves and drove the birds
to silence.

That afternoon I just glanced through a couple of
books, and wrote out a few catalogue cards. That was all
I did in the way of work before I went down and said
'good-bye' and made my way to the park, through the
cool colonnade of black-cottonwood trees to the settlement. The sky was blurred with heat, grey and fluffy at
the edges, and when I climbed the settlement wall, it
burned. The ha-ha was empty, and for the first time I did
not stop there, or pause to stare at the hill.

The nurse on duty lent me a bath-key, without
question, as though she understood the importance of
this occasion, as though I had acquired a new status.
While I was dressing, the Sister came up with a bowl of
apricots, and laid it before me as if I were a queen.

'Madam, one may not go to a party without first
having a supper,' she said, 'and dearie,' she fumbled in
her breast-pocket and drew out a tiny shabby leather
box with Gothic lettering. Inside was a heavy silver
chain, 'wear it if it suits you and if you like it, and if it is a
good party with strong memories, then keep it. I should
be honoured to think of it having such a good, fruitful
use. My father too would be pleased to think . . .' her

voice faltered. 'He gave it to me just before he . . . just before we said good-bye. He would be happy to think...'

It went twice round my neck, and as I fixed it, she examined my well-brushed and pressed grey flannel skirt, and my pink jumper.

'That is good,' she said approvingly, pulling absently at one of the old man's bad stitches. 'I think you will be yourself at this party, and that is always a good thing.'

She came down the ward with me and unlocked the door herself. 'And dearie, I hope that Waterminster Place is a happy place, and that you will find yourself among future friends.'

I took the bus down the avenue into the town. I seemed to fly like a bird. My clothes seemed light and willing to be forgotten; I seemed for once to have them under control.

Waterminster Place was a long, narrow cul-de-sac of tall, double-fronted houses. Helena's aunt, I saw, lived in a top flat and as I mounted the dark flights of stairs my spirits rose in anticipation. I could hear feet shuffling and the sound of bottles being uncorked, and voices everywhere. They spread over the house in a long, low growl of contentment out of which some stood clearly. The gay voice of a man crying:

'Thank you, thank you! Remember I've got to drive. I think, Audrey, I'd better hand my keys over to you here-and-now while I'm still sober...'

And another voice pounding: 'I tell you, no Brains'

Trust will work so long as you've always got to have a gaggle of rudes and silly old sages to balance the bright young men . . .'

'Oh, he's mad about cameras. Talks about nothing except direction, resolution and grain.'

And nearer to me: 'If we were playing draughts, I'd just swallow you up like that,' and a girl's laugh.

'Oh but I like draughts,' she murmured quietly.

'It's Dixieland,' someone called, bending over a gramophone.

I saw Helena in the middle talking to some of Tony's friends:

'Well, we're having the flat done up, but as soon as Tony's contract is settled we shall be off to Rhodesia, only for eighteen months though. We would not dream of settling there and losing all our contacts. If you want to get anywhere these days . . .' she suddenly seemed much older than me, she grimaced. 'Personally I find it all a dreadful bore but there you are, in a competitive world . . .' She caught sight of me: 'Josephine,' she was saying in a small, cool voice, 'we were hoping you'd manage it. We thought when we did not hear from you, that you were too busy. We know you intellectuals don't have much time for this kind of thing. All the nicer to see you. Tony, this is Josephine,' she introduced me in the darkening, smoke-filled room. Someone was lighting candles along the walls. Someone was protesting against Dixieland. 'King Oliver,' he shouted and the music started up again.

'Josephine,' Helena repeated above the noise, 'one of our college "tufts". One of the egg-heads of our year.'

'What did you read?' someone asked politely.

'English,' I replied.

'She had a yen for Anglo-Saxon. I don't know what I would have done without her.'

I shook hands with Tony. He was moving round swiftly, filling people's glasses. He offered me a drink with a pleasant smile, and introduced me into a group of his friends.

At first I was content just to look round the room and listen to the scraps of conversation that popped up all round me. I found myself peering at two girls who were standing together in a corner discussing something. They had bare necks and arms and pale, smooth faces. One had a backless dress; the other had her hair draped round her head like a linen cloth. I gazed enviously. My jumper was hot, and I could feel the heavy, old-fashioned chain tugging at my neck. I decided that as soon as I had received Mrs. Maybury's second monthly cheque, I would go out and buy a dress of smooth lilac tweed, like that, as smooth and straight as the bark of a beech tree.

'Is she still floating round with Brian?' They lowered their voices and whispered. The other nodded.

'He's being rather tough-minded about it actually,' she said confidentially. 'I must show you the photographs I was telling you about.'

She fumbled in her bag, a bag like a white muslin

sunflower that swung lightly at her wrist, and drew out photographs. 'Don't you think it's a good one of me?' she murmured confidentially.

'Yes, awfully,' the linen-head whispered. 'Not very like you, of course, but awfully good. It's so cheeky, and it's got a terrific amount of essay.'

'Yes,' the other one agreed. They bustled round the sunflower bag like a pair of busy mice. 'There's Peter,' one said, and Peter waved, picked up a drink and came over.

With a kind of explosion the room seemed to have filled. There were people everywhere, suddenly larger than life. People standing against the windows; people straddled over armchairs; people perched precariously against tables and shelves, crouching on the floor arguing, or thrusting their heads into clusters and jutting out their chins ready to give out bursts of laughter. In one corner a couple were clutching each other, swaying to 'Lodgin' house Blues', in a very small space; another couple were sitting on the floor sharing a savoury biscuit. It was just as I had imagined the inside of a party would be. There was nothing uncertain or tentative about it; there were no in-between gaps, and I was happy.

'You seem to be taking a very male view of the proceedings, a very detached, philosophic view.'

The man in black whom the two girls called Peter smiled down at me haughtily. He was very tall and thin, and his eyelids were heavy and white, like cream-cheese.

He raised them slowly and let them drop down while he scrutinized me.

'Did you make that?' he pointed at the pink jumper. 'If so it was a jolly good effort for an Anglo-Saxon expert.'

The two little mice squeaked.

'No, I did not make it,' and I began to tell him about the man from Balichery who spent his days knitting jumpers.

He murmured something. His mouth flopped open and shut.

'Sorry,' I said. 'I did not quite catch it.'

It was so noisy, you see. The mice were rustling at my side, and there were suddenly so many mouths opening and shutting and thrusting sounds into the enormous gap that had just opened between this black-suited man and myself.

'Sorry,' I repeated. 'I can't quite hear across the gap.' He repeated himself. He shouted across. I thought he said something about 'callervoyah'.

'I thought you said "callervoyah",' I laughed.

But he only said 'ha!' and shifted his feet up and down in turn. 'Let me fill your glass for you.'

A wave of noise swept us apart, and when I looked again I could see that my glass had been refilled and laid on the mantelpiece beside me, but I could not see the tall haughty young man who had, I thought, said 'callervoyah'.

The talk flowed backwards and forwards, and the

groups shifted and reformed. I seemed to have worked my way through to the other side of the room, like in the game of 'Here we come looby-loo'.

An Indian was leaning against the mantelpiece explaining solemnly to a girl in black why an 'ought' can never follow from an 'is'. Tony bustled up and refilled our glasses and introduced us; Isabel, Josephine, Kurshnan. Kurshnan was reading P.P.E. at Oxford. He smiled slightly and repeated his argument, his voice rising higher and higher as though we were going to disagree with him. He beat his pipe against the mantelpiece to emphasize his rightness.

But Isabel only laughed, and cried:

'Is that so? Is that so? Well, I never.' She was small and pale and slightly Cockney, with a long fringe of dark hair. 'Is that so?' She hid her face in her hands and laughed. 'But you'll never prove to me that God doesn't exist.'

'You can never make existence a predicate.' Kurshnan rapped severely. 'Predicates divide things into classes . . .'

'Really, is that so?'

Isabel tittered and turned to me:

'My mind,' she grinned, 'if you ever wanted to draw a picture of it, you would have to put in lots of foliage everywhere. Leaves and greenery, that's always the way when I try to think. But then, I read Modern Languages. They should really be done at technical colleges, not Universities.'

The air was thick and blue with smoke. Someone

went to the window, abruptly drew back the curtain, and threw the window up. The night outside was a pale silvery blue, and here we all were, four flights up, floating in a kind of hammock in all that blue, talking about 'is's' and 'oughts'. I could see eyes behind Isabel's, heads moving and twisting, mouths opening and shutting and receiving liquid and savoury biscuit. No one seemed to think it was at all a surprising situation to be in.

'What do you do?' Isabel was saying. I told her about the catalogue of books.

'Of flowers or fruit, or the higher virtues or what?'

'Of everything. Everything there is.'

She pulled a face. 'And what did you get? What degree, I mean?'

'I never took schools. I was ill.'

'Oh, poor darling!' a rich voice broke in from the group of people who were behind us. A pair of large grey eyes gazed at me. 'Did you get one of those merciless *aegrotats* where you have to present yourself in all your illness to the Dean in full "subfusc" and say something in Latin which you cannot even remember? Robin told me of a friend of his . . .' she turned to a tired, anxious-looking man, with heavy, dark-rimmed eyes, who was staring at her. She waited for him to continue the story, but he stood silent. I noticed he was slightly bald.

'Darling,' he said in a whisper, 'we ought to be going.'

She sighed. She wore a pleated dress, the colour of honey, that whistled when she moved. 'You see, we've left Paul – he's only a year – with Miss West who's down below. She's a dear, but she plays the violin, not fearfully well, unfortunately, and it makes Paul howl. I always wanted to cry too when my sister learned the violin. It was only afterwards that I learned that Vitali's "Gavotte" was not something terribly deep and searching and soulful . . . so I've always been off the violin, and I suppose Paul has inherited it . . .'

Her husband was urging her with whispers. 'Alison, we ought . . .' But Alison seemed anxious to stay there, balancing a glass by its delicate stem in the warm pool of light among the smiling faces. The noise seemed to shut everything out except the present moment and that was kind.

'Has anyone seen John, John Hope lately?' she asked.

'He's off on his travels again, Alison, you may be sure. Sniffing out adventure in Tunisia I think.'

'He seems to have a good nose for adventure,' her husband noted heavily and dutifully.

Alison smiled. 'I'm all for adventure.'

'I like adventure too,' I broke in. 'I once followed the line of the Thames and Severn Canal until it went under a hill.' They were all listening. 'It was a very strange experience,' I tried to explain to them, 'because in most places it had disappeared, just died, and there was nothing left to mark it but a line of rushes.'

'Really?' asked someone. 'How sad.'

'How sinister!' shuddered Alison. Her husband shifted his feet and looked at her lovingly.

I went on. They seemed waiting for me to go on. 'In

one place there is only a red stone arch left, in the middle
of a field of barley. That's all that's left to mark the
canal that once carried cargoes and big ships to the
very heart of England.'

'Horrible!' she shuddered again.

There it was. I could see the canal running away
towards the Golden Valley, with the round, flaking
plaster towers which once marked the locks. I remembered the boy who had run out of one of them with a dog
to drive me off, and had stopped to tell me proudly of the
ships that had once sailed to Gloucester under that hill.
And now there were only a few empty towers and beds
of green rushes. 'So you see,' I ended, 'that adventure
made me rather sad.'

Alison nodded sympathetically. 'There's a canal like
that at home, and when they drained it, it gave me the
creeps, like seeing a venerable person undressed . . .'

We all laughed. I seemed to be in the heart of this
group of talking people. I had even forgotten the blue
night outside.

'Another adventure . . .' I began again luxuriously.

'John's last adventure,' someone interrupted, 'was a
delicious Arab with a whiff of the slave-trade. I believe
she was even veiled when he first met her.' There was
more laughter. 'Trust him!'

The gap seemed suddenly to have reappeared round
me. They were talking about 'purdah' now. The Indian
was expounding a theory of descriptions, leaning against
an alabaster vase that tipped and creaked in response to

his vehemence. The girl in black called Isabel had started to dance in one corner of the room, half by herself, half holding on to a man.

'Darling,' Alison's husband was whispering timidly, 'we've got to think of Paul and the violin.'

Alison smiled reluctantly. They looked for Helena and Tony. Then they disappeared and I seemed to be alone in the space, in a kind of channel that I did not seem able to stretch out of. At the bottom a middle-aged lady sat on a settee talking in a deep, brisk voice. Her legs stuck out like pegs in front of her, hardly meeting the floor. I went over to avoid being in the channel. She smiled vaguely at me as she talked.

It was about engagements, weddings, daughters-in-law. 'I suggested to my future daughter-in-law,' she was saying, 'that we might have a round of golf together to improve her play (and I wanted to get to know her too!). At last she did come round, but only to confess rather shamefacedly that actually she would prefer to take colour-photographs of the garden. Apparently she adored flowers. Well, I did eventually coax her round, but when I at last located her, she wasn't in the garden, but *asleep* on the settee in the drawing-room! So much for my future daughter-in-law's golf. Fortunately it has been broken off, so I still don't know her form.'

Helena had appeared at the other side of the settee, smiling at us all. They were asking her about Tony's and her plans. She grimaced and shrugged, deprecatingly. 'This is all frightfully tedious and parochial. Wait till it catches up on you,' she nodded at me, and began to tell us of the completely unspoilt place they were going to off the foot of Italy.

'Never go for a honeymoon,' a tall woman next to me whispered. 'I spent a fortnight on the floor of a hotel near Calne. My husband had a passion for Wiltshire; said the hills were a different shape and talked about nothing but sarsens, for three weeks. But that floor was hard! I didn't sleep a wink the whole time. But still, you're supposed to come back from a honeymoon looking...'

'Oh, it was a management course,' Helena was saying reluctantly. 'Three months on the belt first of all, getting practical experience. But when I had spent four months on the line, filling cardboard boxes with threepenny chocolate bars (and they gave you cocoa at eleven and chocolate blancmange at lunch) I complained that I would be round the bend if I did not get some kind of change and promotion. The supervisor was rather flustered and promised me a change, and put me on *sixpenny* bars instead of *threepenny*. Same old cardboard boxes, but sixpenny bars.'

'So you got engaged instead.'

'The only way out.'

'They were off to Rhodesia, as good a place as any to start off in,' the aunt was saying firmly. 'We were out there nearly twenty years. I think Helena and Tony will make a go of it. Money is all right. Plenty of service and no domestic problems. Personally I loathed the snakes.

They were my worst scare. I never got used to them.
I used to send the boys round every night with sticks and
lanterns. An awful performance, but that's all part of the
game, isn't it? Poor Ronnie was bitten by a crocodile
and his wife had a nervous breakdown as the result,
and never recovered, but still . . .'

On the other side they were still talking about golf.
I seemed to be floating just a little way out, a little way
away from both groups.

'Perhaps you don't play?' the golfers were asking
me.

'Play?'

'Golf.'

But I saw that I was still among the scrubby roots of
the tobacco plant, and watching the Persian gazelle, the
Rhodesian spiny mouse, and the diced water snake.
'Play?'

There was the problem of Julia's Fugitive Snake.
No one could discover its longevity, I remembered
lovingly. It was a mystery. Compared with man's
longevity or even the diced water snake's . . . I specu-
lated, while the talk spread all round me like spilled water
leaking into every corner. It seemed to include every
topic except the longevity of Julia's Fugitive Snake.

It was so hot. I could feel sweat trickling down my
face. The music blared and stopped. Faces popped on and
off like lamps. Mouths clapped up and down; words
shot in and out, but the room full of people seemed to
have escaped me. I could not reach in to it. I tried to

stretch out and get caught up in it, but each time my turn came to lay a contribution I found myself catapulted into this empty space in the middle of nothing, discussing with no one but myself the longevity of badgers or Myra's thorny spider.

I looked for Alison. I remembered she had gone. I stumbled towards the door looking for my host and hostess and the light jacket I had brought with me. It was dark on the landing, and I seemed to have been pushed instead into another room where they were dancing. The light was swinging near the floor sending only a small, sharp circle of light on to the lino. There were several couples spread over the floor talking and smoking.

I was just about to make my apologies for gate-crashing, and slip out and bide my time quietly in the passage outside, when someone thin and dark and hungry, with a surly, reluctant smile pointed to a place beside him on a chair and I did not like to refuse. But it was one of those circular chairs, and rather uncomfortable for two. After sitting there for a bit I began to grow rather bored. I sat on my half and tried not to encroach on the gentleman. But there was not really very much room, and my partner seemed to take up more than his fair share, and I had to hold my breath in order to avoid pressing my arm into his side. I grew even hotter as he talked about his biochemical research – I imagined he must be at one of the (what Mother would call) more democratic universities. I kept having to shift a little as there were pins and needles beginning to come in my arm.

'Come and dance,' he mumbled at last. 'There's more room now.' He clasped me round the waist. But I did not know what to do with my arms. They hung out like the arms of a perambulator. 'Put them round my neck,' he hissed frowning. 'No, not like that, and don't apologize.'

The music swayed backwards and forwards on one note. I was rather uncomfortable in my arms, trying not to lean with all my weight lest I should press into him.

'Why so tense?' he murmured. 'Just relax.'

'I am afraid I can't dance,' I confessed.

'You don't have to.' He squeezed my waist, and then put his hands on my neck. 'Nice smooth skin.'

'It would be easier if I had some roller-skates,' I murmured sadly, seeing that I would never dance. 'Then you could just wheel me.'

He was still pressing me against him. Perhaps there was a specific purpose in the manœuvres. Perhaps the gentleman was an athlete flexing and toning up and so on.

'Are you an athlete?' I asked. 'Are you in training and so on?'

He was stroking my neck and the sides of my cheeks again. 'Nice smooth skin.'

'That's three times you've said it. Is your father a taxidermist or something? You seem to have a special interest.' But whether he was or not I told him I was going to sneeze if he touched me just there. I always did.

Apparently there was a friend whom he had not seen for

several years, and that he must go and say 'hallo.' 'But I can see that you are much more interested in British foreign policy and the things of the mind than in dancing.' He waved to his friend and disappeared.

I was hot and dizzy. I saw that I would never transform my pink jumper and heavy skirt. They were dragging me down. I sank on to a cushion and looked out of the window and saw the pale blue of the night again, and the stars. I stared and I laughed. Isabel was standing there with her partner.

'She makes catalogues of everything there is,' she told him.

'Really?' he bent down politely, 'and what is there? I should like to know.'

They bent towards me, staring, and I began, sitting in the middle of the floor looking out on to the night:

'Well, on the one side, there are the stars and snow, and love, only that's not easy; and death, but that is simpler. And then on the other side there are houses like this one, perched up in the sky, with pockets of electricity and water and music, and pipes and tubes running down into the earth, and everyone eating savouries and dancing and talking about the best way of life, and the way to deal with Rhodesian snakes, all as though nothing had happened. And really it is . . . unbelievable, it is . . .' I appealed to Isabel because the word could not be found. But she and her partner only looked embarrassed. They started dancing again.

'Tell me what it is next time,' she laughed.

Helena was standing by the door talking to Tony. She was biting her lips. I wondered what was wrong. Perhaps it was myself, sitting there in the middle of the floor alone, clutching my knees and searching for the word to describe the feat up here. I tried to speak again, but it felt wrong. My mouth did not feel my own. I saw I was not gracing the party and I got up.

'I must be going,' I murmured sheepishly.

'Must you really?' Helena pulled a long face. 'How sad for us. We've hardly seen you!' while Tony chimed in:

'Oh, surely not! It's but the third hour!'

'It's my bath-night, you see,' I choked.

'And we've hardly seen you yet!'

The music came loudly. They were beginning to dance again. Tony was holding out my jacket for me.

'That's all right,' I began, but she went on:

'Too bad that you've got to be off just now. Just as all the people we had to invite because we "owed", were moving off. Too bad, and I haven't had time to get you in a corner,' she sighed, 'and hear all your news. Just as we were getting going, you have to be off.'

I put my jacket on. 'We are so anxious not to lose touch,' she went on. 'Tony wants to meet you again badly. After Oxford one loses touch with ideas. We weary bread-and-butter plodders don't really appreciate our lions such as you. How is the *Ormulum*?'

She opened the door. As we went down, I heard Tony's voice:

'Oh, someone Helena invited in one of her manic moods. We didn't really think she'd turn up though.'

'Not exactly one of the Balliol climbers!'

There was a titter of laughter.

Helena began quickly, 'It's lovely to see you again and I'm looking forward to hearing some more of your existential theories of life. You make me feel ashamed of leading such a non-academic existence. You must come round some time and we'll have a real set-to in the old college style. Do ring! You've got our number.'

We were making a careful ritual progress to the door as she spoke. The stairs welcomed me down into their darkness. I glided down as though I were in a lift. The party was over, though it sounded from the noise upstairs as though it would not be over for a long time. It was just my début into the real world that was done.

There was laughter all round me, laughter following me as I made my way down into the kind darkness, across the square, through the town and up the avenue that led to the settlement. The night was young, indeed it had hardly begun up there at Waterminster Place.

I stared at the stars as I drifted up the hill towards the boundaries of the town, and a strange lightness came over me, as though I did not really exist. The stars that had seemed so bright as I peered from the lighted room seemed to be no more now than little bits of paper cut out and clipped up there. The houses, 'Cranmere', 'St. Briavels' and the 'Neuk' might have been painted on a flapping canvas, and my feet made a queer light tapping sound on the paving-stones as though they were not feet but only rubber-pointed crutch-ends, tap-tapping up the hill that was so straight, into the night. I might go on tap-tapping for ever up the hill, and it would make no difference to anyone. No one would be any the wiser if I pressed on for ever.

I had reached the arcade of shops half-way up the hill, and the rows of slot-machines that served out cigarettes. I looked at their eyes and mouths, but they were silent, and would confirm or deny nothing. I wanted to shout and hear a reply. I called 'cooee', but the long avenue remained empty and silent. There was nothing, nothing to tell me that I existed. My voice, like my feet, was light, without weight, like paper. I drifted back to the settlement.

I got slowly undressed. I took off the clanking silver chain and dropped it in a vase from Torquay. The rose had already fallen leaving only a safety-pin pinching a lump of wool. I got into bed and lay there hearing the music that I had not danced to; the talk that I had not taken part in, and the straight line of the avenue that seemed to go on for ever. And then there was the laughter, laughter, higher and higher, but on the top of it all was Alasdair's laughter.

I tossed and turned, neither asleep nor awake. I could neither wake up nor fall asleep. There were two sides to everything, I knew. If I turned over I might reach the other side. But the voices and music intervened and thrust themselves between, and I lay there suspended.

Then I was suddenly properly awake. Something was clicking and creaking outside, but it was not the wind. I climbed on to the window-sill and looked out. The gentle crying of the music and the sounds of laughter had left me now and the pale blue had gone from the sky. Instead there was a dirty, low-lying grey, and the shrubs were creaking with a load on their leaves. The summer had broken, and it was raining. It was morning as well, and the nurses were singing as they banged along the corridor throwing open the doors, and calling, 'Good morning, good morning.'

I buried my head in the darkness of the blanket and hid from the sounds of the Sister's morning greeting:

'So was it a happy party? Was Waterminster Place a happy place, my dear?'

I wanted the knack of existing. I did not know the rules.

Chapter Five

THE NEXT day the world filled slowly with rain. It was the first for nearly two months, and everything was wrapped in a film of grey-green. It hung there like a screen before the summer world, and I wanted to run behind it and regain the dry landscape where I had been happy. I wanted to run behind it and hide from the Sister's cries that followed me everywhere that Saturday:

'Josephine, Josephine, was it a good party? Was Waterminster Place a happy place, dearie?'

The rain crackled on the roof all morning, like a bubbling pan, and then in the afternoon it changed to fine spray that floated down from the hill like powder while the kind voice still pursued me relentlessly:

'Josephine! Josephine!' down the long corridor, across the gallery, through the locker-room, gently mocking me. 'Josephine, how did the dreamer find the big world?' the passionate voice hunted me down.

I hid from it in the wash-room. I bent over the hot pipes tearing strips of wet rag, and binding them tighter and tighter round the pipes till the steam rose up in my face. The gong went for lunch. I leaned there against the long, bleared windows, hearing the trees creaking with their load of wet; and watching the gardens grow greener and greener, and the roofs turn black and shiny like tar.

The gong went for supper; I was hungry. But as I passed the clinical room going towards the gallery where cold meat was laid out on Saturday evenings for those who had returned from their day off, the Sister caught me. She was leaning over a glass trolley and her hands were fumbling with a hypodermic syringe, but she looked up sharply as I passed, as though she were only waiting there for me, and called out:

'Well dearie, I want to hear all about your new friends.' I stood still in the doorway. She waited, the needle suspended in her hand. 'Are they the kind of young people among whom you would wish to make your life, when you leave us?' The syringe clattered down against the glass tray. She looked at me. There was a little crumb trembling on her cheek, just above her mouth. From her tea, I supposed. Or could she have taken an early supper? 'Then . . .' she paused expectantly, 'how is it?'

I opened my mouth. I tried to laugh as I had seen them laugh, throwing back my head and exclaiming that it had been a gorgeous party, glorious, 'whack on'.

'I . . . I . . . ' I began. 'It . . . '

The wind blew against the net curtain. The gas-fire hissed. A smell of chloroform came up from the needle and wads of cotton-wool. I happened to be pinned to that clinical scene at that particular moment. But it was just chance, and as for the party, nothing was real at all.

'I . . . I . . . ' I struggled. But nothing happened. Talking about Waterminster Place, I thought, was like paying a bill in money that was not mine. It was as though I had no right to mention the world of Helena and Prue and Tony as though it were mine. I mumbled something shamefacedly, staring at the dark green lino floor and the black cylinders of oxygen.

She had covered the glass trolley carefully with a cloth, and was rolling it towards the door. It squeaked shrilly as it ran. She stopped thoughtfully:

'So,' she said gently. 'There is much to say, and,' she screwed up her eyes, 'life is a coin that has two sides, a reverse and an obverse. Shall I come to your salon for audience when I come off duty tonight? Shall I? Yes? I very much would like to hear about the outer world. I have lived most of my life on the inside, remember?'

I mumbled an assent. She clapped a mask over her face, and the trolley squeaked down to the dormitory. But when I saw that the rain had stopped I persuaded the ward-maid to lend me her key, and escaped into the gardens.

There was no one about. The last car went down the
drive, and the cats scuttled among the laurel bushes
shaking showers of water from the leaves. In the day-
room of the refractory ward they were singing 'Onward
Christian Soldiers', grappling with it so fiercely that they
drowned the erratic, staccato piano. A sudden burst of
crying came out; the nurse's footsteps and the jingle of
keys. The piano lid came down with a bang, and there
was silence.

I leaned against a beech tree and tried to think. I
wondered what words were *the words*, the things that
carried, the words that counted, and qualified you for the
world of other people. I saw why Mrs. Maybury was
puzzled, why, standing in the doorway, she always left
the gap, always paused, waiting for me to say something
about myself, my life, my friends, what I did, where I
belonged, so that she could place me somewhere in the
world that she was familiar with. And I had thought
I was happy because the past was over. But the past it
seemed was never over; the gulf was never bridged
between then and now.

I stood in the empty wet twilight waiting. I supposed I
was waiting, but I was not certain what for: perhaps for
someone to walk down the path between the beech trees
towards me, to bear down on me, and claim me. I stood
and waited under the dripping trees, just in case someone
should come, but the only person who came towards me
was a small boy in a cowboy shirt who had been talking
to his mother at the window.

'You got the time?' he asked uncuriously, fiddling with a rusty pen-nib.

It was almost dark when I got back to the drive. There was no light left upon the ground. I could see a shadow moving about in the box at the main doors. It was the receptionist standing there, talking over her shoulder to someone, powdering her nose, sliding her coat round her and saying good night. As she clipped out and slammed the door behind her, she turned and smiled and I saw that she had been talking to Alasdair. He had been leaning there talking and smoking against the counter of the wooden hutch.

He blew out smoke and smiled at me. 'Nine-thirty!' He pulled a long face. 'Another two hours to kill. What's the next move? I seem to be propping today up! How do you manage these nunnery hours of yours?'

He looked at me expectantly but I had nothing to say. 'I shan't sleep,' he sighed, 'unless something steps in to break up this monotonous, virtuous calm.'

'It has stopped raining,' I suggested dully. 'At least almost, except for the dripping from the trees. And there is a piece of the moon out. Like someone's fingernail,' I added. 'If you'll excuse me . . .'

'*La Lune ne garde aucune rancune*,' he murmured. 'The easiest way to sleep, of course, is to exhaust one's emotions. I used to know someone who went round provoking people deliberately in the hopes of being provoked. It acted as a kind of tranquillizer only unfortunately the English make a point of not being provoked . . .' he broke off. 'Good party?' tilting his head back and staring at me. 'Did you remember to smile nicely? And was there plenty to drink? And,' he pulled a wry face, 'did you remember to put a dress on?'

I saw that underneath his face he was laughing. Perhaps he had been laughing all along.

'Why did you send me to that place, that party?' I croaked. 'I don't belong anywhere except here.'

We were standing in the main reception hall. A little light came in from outside, a horrible purple and green light, grimly through the leaded panes. The hall smelt of stew and cleansers, and up above the seats for visitors, the notices and the potted plants in rows along the gaudy tiled floors, were huge metal wheels that ground when you turned them, and wound open the windows secretly and slowly away up in the domed roof. The place was an institution, I saw, a place for the remnants and the droppings of society.

Alasdair was turning the wheel, pretending to be a sea-captain, and laughing as the loathsome windows up above our heads creaked open an inch with a grim whisper. He was talking about something, but he stopped sharply and looked surprised when I burst into tears.

'Sorry old thing. Awfully sorry. This is bad.' He held out his packet of cigarettes. 'Are you fed up about this business?' He was gently jogging my elbow. 'Is it something you can tell to Uncle Alasdair? Here, let's have a smoke.'

'Let's have a smoke,' he was repeating, 'and we can talk. We'll stay outside the morgue for a bit, if it will help.'

I saw him leading me down the wide mosaic corridor where the patients did not go except by summons. No one seemed to raise any objection, though, as we penetrated the official world. The nurses who passed as they went off duty just smiled and said 'Good evening, Mr. Faber', as though he were a familiar figure there.

We went past the offices, all in darkness, the kitchens where big tins were being rattled and stacked; past the treatment rooms, the sewing rooms, and the Matron's sitting-room.

'Where are we?' I asked. 'Where are we going?' Passages suddenly spread round us like spokes of a wheel.

'Just to find somewhere to be away from neurosis for half an hour,' and he caught hold of my arm, and drew me away to the right.

I did not ask any more where we were going in the darkness. It was sufficient to be drawn along by the elbow, for it assured me that at least something existed; at least something was real, even if it was only my arm being drawn along, and something at the other end of it, leading me.

I was lulled. I shut my eyes. I bumped into one of the enormous window-wheels that jutted out of the wall.

'What are you playing at?' Alasdair turned kindly as we turned a corner and I knocked against the wall. 'What's the game?'

'I'm pretending I am blind and you are leading me.'

'Is that good?'

I nodded.

'Significant, I'm sure,' he said. 'Some sort of Freudian symbolism in plotting to bump into a bannister, but I'm not quite sure what.' We climbed a flight of stairs. At the top we stopped. 'Shall we go into the board-room?'

That was where the committee met, where the doctors had their case-conferences and, I suppose, where they regraded people and put them on trial. He led me along a passage that was carpeted and smelt of scented soap, and then we halted. I opened my eyes.

It was a long, dark room the shape of a half-moon with bay windows down the curved side. A lamp shone in from a bracket in the wall outside, and lit up one side-wall. We stood in the doorway and peered in cautiously. The room was empty.

There was a long table down the middle, with chairs scattered round it as though a conference had just been abandoned. We crept in and wandered round the table to the window. There was a smell of dusty carpets, and the harsh, sour smell from ashtrays. From the wall at the end the founder stared down at us uncompromisingly.

'Wow!' said Alasdair. 'He obviously doesn't like the look of us. Shrewd chap!'

All along the other wall there were bookshelves:

Intra-cranial Tumours, Legal aspects of Psychosis, Twenty Cases of Lobotomy, ran the titles, lit up by the lamp outside. We turned our backs on them and went and sat down at the two armchairs that headed the long board-room table.

'Order, order,' Alasdair called, 'Mr. Alasdair Faber, an interesting case of conversion-hysteria . . . gentle-men . . .' He stopped abruptly and we just sat there with the square lamp-bracket outside sending in a yellow light into this old, private, rambling part of the hospital.

'Well,' Alasdair cried, breaking the silence at length by pushing his chair aside and sliding to the floor, 'shall we sit and tell sad stories of the deaths of kings . . . ?' I suppose he caught the expression on my face, because he stopped abruptly and gave one of his grimaces. 'So the party was dismal. Never mind! Better luck next time!'

'It wasn't the party that was wrong. It was me.'

'Oh.' He drew up his knees and smoked. There was something comforting in the way the red glow of his cigarette went in and out, and smoke puffed into the air. 'Not your type perhaps,' but he did not seem at all surprised. 'Hard luck. Poor old thing. The *tête à tête* is your medium, I expect.'

'You asked me once why I was here and I couldn't tell you.' I trembled. 'But now I see why – after going to the party I see what's wrong. It's because I don't belong anywhere else. I don't know the rules of life, and if I kept a phrase-book for twenty years I would not know the right answers. It's a thing I shall never learn. I am odd, incorrect, illegitimate. You see, I'm . . .' my voice was rising higher and higher, 'I must be illegitimate.'

I was crying again. The wet was bouncing off my hands on to the table and then to the carpet.

'What does it matter,' he smiled coolly, 'eh? Marriage is only legalized rape. It's only a convention . . .'

I seemed to be crying more because he did not understand. 'Here, come here,' he said, patting his pocket for his handkerchief. 'This is rather torrential.'

'I don't mind legally,' I chattered, 'I should not mind that so much. It's the other kind I mean. My eyes are always turned in the wrong direction. My thoughts are always on the wrong things. I'm not a proper person at all. I'm one of those who ought never to have been born, or wasn't born or, or . . . something like that.'

'That sounds hard.' He pulled a long face, and rubbed his hands slowly down the sides of his nose deliberately, and put them over his mouth. 'That must be very disconcerting, very disqualifying. No wonder you didn't enjoy the party. But you know, frankly, I didn't really think you would . . .'

I waited. I was puzzled. It was, after all, he who had urged me to go to the party. 'Why did you think I wouldn't enjoy it then?'

'Well, just for the reasons you've said. Detached people like you don't usually find it easy to make the right kind of contact . . . at least . . .' he drummed casually on his knee, 'that particular kind of illness . . . at least I don't know. It's only what I've learned from the male nurses and reading Meyer-Gros's book, and watching and talking to the schizies on the ward.' He opened his mouth as though he could snatch back and swallow what he had said.

'What?' I asked, 'what was that?'

There was a horrible silence while I stared, waiting for him to repeat himself.

'Sorry,' he snapped out. 'Sorry. Forget it. I know nothing, actually, about the subject.' He looked angry and stubbed out his half-smoked cigarette. But I had not forgotten our first conversation by the ha-ha.

'Is that what they call schizophrenia then? Is that what's wrong with me?' I asked. The books behind us seemed to be shouting out: 'Twenty cases of Lobotomy' . . . what came next?

'Oh forget it,' he repeated anxiously. 'I know nothing about nervous and functional disorders.' He frowned at the ground. 'All I meant was that reflective, serious people like yourself respond best in small groups of people not in big galaxic crowds where everyone is forced to be as empty as possible about everything.'

There was a long pause. He relit his cigarette. He was still frowning. 'Forget what I said,' he repeated, patting and fidgeting with his socks. 'I'm really entirely ignorant, I assure you.'

There was another long pause while I thought. I could only hear his breathing in and out, and the nervous tapping of his cigarette. At last he whispered:

'Do you mind? It's only *their* terminology, after all. It's only a word. It's only one way of saying that you are more real than most people, more involved in the fundamentals of existence. O.K.?' He detached his hand from his socks and brought it over to my arm and fingered the cuff of my velvet jacket and smiled, 'O.K.?'

I did not feel O.K. at all, but I nodded, and we sat there for a long time. I remembered how the Sister had warned me not to be frightened of labels, but her injunctions had seemed irrelevant then. The world had seemed too real and too pressing for me to be bothered about labels. But now the books behind us had a sudden and ominous weight as though they might fall forward and suffocate me. 'You think it's all a disease?' I asked in a half-strangled voice. 'Shall I ever be cured properly?'

'You *are* cured,' he said firmly. 'A jolly good recovery.' He was still pulling at his chin and patting the leg of the table alternately with some anxiety. 'Jolly sorry to be so tactless. The clinical level is very superficial after all. You know,' he went on, seeing I suppose that I was still staring abstractedly at yesterday and the two months of fool's paradise that preceded this revelation. 'You know,' he took a deep breath, laughed gently and blew smoke towards the ceiling, 'far from being, as you suggest, an awful bastard, you are about the most legitimate, the most real person I have ever met.'

'Am I? What do you mean?' I stared stupidly.

'Come here. Come and sit here,' he patted the carpet beside him under the table and I slithered from my chair to the floor beside him, and leaned propped against the table-leg while he sprawled on one elbow beside it. I would at that moment have obeyed any instructions.

'I repeat,' he whispered; his voice had become softer and gentler, 'you are the first person I have ever met, the first woman at any rate, who does not just play a game with herself and other people. You say you don't know the rules, and can't learn them. But that is what is so nice about you. You are real, you are serious. You aren't just playing a game as other women are.'

He looked at me with his funny grimace, half smile, half deprecation. 'Parties aren't the ideal background for serious people.'

'No,' I said mechanically, and waited.

'It's not because you are schizophrenic . . . that's just a goddamn silly word . . . but because you are real that "society" in the common sense of the word doesn't appeal to you much. That's what I like about you. I admired you for that reason the very first time I saw you, sitting all alone in that ditch with your hair flying and no make-up on and not bothering about what people thought of you. You refreshed me. You do good to people like me who lead rather empty lives. Do you still mind the label?'

'It depends,' I replied cautiously. 'How do I do you good?'

'Some people give me the creeps. They are so terrifyingly, so diabolically correct and proper. I've seen lots of them. They make me go cold. I want to run away when I think of them. Guilt, I suppose really. I've let so many of that tribe down, and perhaps I have a tendency that way myself.'

'You think it does not matter then, being odd, and not belonging anywhere?'

'My dear, you ought to be thankful, not miserable, that you are not like Helena What's-it-What's-it, I assure you. I don't mean that their lives stink. They are probably quite worthy and useful. It's just that they are so busy finding husbands, and houses and good income brackets that they just haven't time to be conscious.' He grinned anxiously. 'O.K.?'

The more silent and thoughtful I became the more urgently and pressingly he talked.

'It's only another way of saying,' he was breathless with talking and kept looking at me out of the corner of his eye as he repeated it for the fourth or fifth time, 'that you are more *real* than most people. It's not sex that divides the human race in two, but this awful splendid quality of having it all taped. Mind you, I think the religious people are just as bad at this as anyone else. It's the awful power of possession, of seeing the world as an inventory, a container of so many things, and other people as so many tin-openers to undo it for you. It's all so stuffy, so anaesthetized, so damn unreal.'

'Is that your illness as well then?'

'I think that is what paralysed me and sent me impotent and all-that-that-I-won't-go-into-details-about... Wow, I'm becoming like the jolly old Delphic Oracle,' he wound up at length. 'But I assure you they give me the creeps too.'

He was still there sitting over his knees, searching for some more to say. But he need not have bothered, for I was laughing. I was sprawling over the carpet laughing. 'You needn't look so anxious,' I assured him. 'I don't mind at all.' I was asking myself why I had ever wanted, even for two hours on a Friday evening, to squeeze myself out of the real experiences that were mine, into a box that did not fit. For as I sat there thinking of the party and the conversations I had listened to, and tried to take part in, in that strange, brittle atmosphere four flights up in the sky, it was they who became unreal, and what the textbooks could mean by schizophrenia was only that whereas most flies crawl along the ceiling in a well-behaved, decorous posture talking about the other sex, or income tax allowances or the articles of faith that ought to be taught in prep-schools, some see how things really are on the ceiling, upside down, and get anxious and frightened, or want to laugh at the incongruity and oddness of that fantastic position. 'I never was cured and I never shall be,' I protested.

'What are you laughing at?' Alasdair asked anxiously, for I was still rolling on the carpet laughing.

'We are flies,' I cried. 'We are flies! I too feel prophetic and Delphic! Some are well-mannered and walk along the ceiling talking about the rearing of children or *art brut*, or the property laws. But it's absurd. The posture's absurd, absurd!'

'Have a heart,' he whispered, because I was shouting, and then: 'I've never seen you like that before,' he confessed in his normal voice, falling back on his elbow. 'I like you when you laugh like that. You know, I've never seen you relaxed. I've never seen you spontaneous before. It makes you look nice, like a cat.'

'What do I usually look like then, and how have I changed?' I challenged him. I looked into his eyes for the first time perhaps. We stared.

'It's come alive. Your face has lost its deadpan look. In fact you've *got* a face.' He paused and started as though he had made a discovery. 'You know, I believe you are human after all.'

'Human? Did you think I was a monster or a barbarian or something from another planet when we sat on the bench in the summer?' The summer seemed far away. I remembered that it was only yesterday. I stretched out under the table.

He was stretched out too. A cloud of pleasant smoke seemed to have crept down round us. The staring founder and the books about mental disease seemed to be outside, and inside it was warm. I was beside him, almost leaning against him.

'Not bad,' he was saying in his normal tone again. 'You might even learn to be flippant and *frivole*.' He giggled, 'I might even teach you to be a little bit flirtatious.' He touched my wrist and shook it. 'Would you like to learn, eh?' I nodded.

We met every night of that rainy week. Every night

as the day staff disappeared and the night staff came cycling up the drive shouting expansively to each other about their husbands and children, we went to the board-room and sat there under the long table and no one troubled us.

Alasdair would put his arm round my shoulders as we talked, and gradually draw me on top of him, and I would lie there as it grew dark with the lamp-bracket outside sending a fistful of light on to the rows of books that I had learned to despise, comforted and assured, in some strange way I had never anticipated, that, enclosed within a strong circle, I existed. There was that aura surrounding people, and I had never stood within it before.

'Let's go then, eh?' he would raise his eyebrow, and we would steal downstairs, across the tennis courts and beech-walk, over the rough grass that was now spongy and wet, across the ha-ha, and over the wall.

It seemed a different town when we went there together in the dark, and sat in a pub or a coffee bar, with a juke-box playing the kind of music that before this I had only overheard.

One night we went to a cinema; one night we saw people dancing and jiving in a cellar down by our feet, and as we stared through the wire-netting area down on to their faces, Alasdair smiled:

'Shall we go down? Let's dance. What do you say?'

'I can't dance. I've never been to a . . .' But I did not have to dance. We just clung to each other swaying to the rhythm of the music in the crushed, stifling atmosphere of the cellar-room. My spirits soared at this assault on life.

'You've done me good, you know,' he told me several times as we made our way back, hot and breathless with hurrying. 'You've reminded me that another world exists. Nice little thing. You are good in the "Kleinean" sense. How have you managed to retain your innocence?'

I tried to describe my life with Mother, and the strange remote world I had belonged to and how the hospital had intervened to end that.

'At least, not the hospital, but you. You make me feel real. You have taken me out of the fowler's snare.'

'Thank you. I'm glad I've performed such a useful function. Perhaps I shall have a few days off purgatory for that.'

We were standing by the main doors. Just over our heads in the tower the clock struck eleven. 'We must push off,' he whispered, 'or we shall be getting the bag. Cat's face, nice little thing, I shall miss you.'

'Miss me? Are you going? Just that?' I seemed for a moment to come off the ground.

'*Lente, lente currite equites nocti,*' he murmured. 'The one tag I remember. Hope I've got it right.' He stretched out his hand and played with a lock of my hair. He took my left hand and put it behind my back. He took the other one and put it behind him, and drew me towards him and pressed his chin into my neck. I felt his rough cheek on my chin, inhaled his breath and the smell of his neck and his jacket, and fumbled towards that thing, strange and dark and opposite, that made me feel so good.

'Are you going?' I struggled towards it. 'You're not going.'

He shook his head. 'Not unless . . . Shall we?' he was whispering. 'Would you like to? Where shall I take you tomorrow?'

Tomorrow was Sunday, just a week since we had discovered the board-room and I had started to discover myself.

'Somewhere dark and far,' I blundered, groping. 'Strange and dark and far and opposite.'

'Tomorrow?' I whispered as we separated at the empty reception box.

'Tomorrow as ever was,' Alasdair replied gaily. 'Half-eleven at the bus stop.'

The ward was in darkness. I felt strong and light-headed as I glided along. I seemed to have acquired solidity, edges and boundaries. I felt like a queen. I crept past the empty office, and past the dormitory where the night nurse was sitting heaped and solitary like a toad in a pool of light among the sleeping bodies.

I glided to my room. I did not bother to switch the light on or to wash. I flung my clothes off, dropped them to the floor, fell straight into bed, and lay there solid and square and smiling.

The moon leaped over the sky. The stars bulged down. I stretched the length of the earth. I was as small and folded as an ant. I must have lain for hours before I fell asleep, but all the time I was smiling at the reality that seemed to be taking shape before me.

Chapter Six

I WOKE UP early and went down to the ha-ha. Damp leaves were beginning to fill it, and spread along the grass and cling to the wall. The air was cold and misty and the sky was white and motionless. It was one of those solemn, still days when momentous decisions are made, when patients are taken away to have brain operations, or when people die.

'Good,' Alasdair murmured as I approached the bus stop in the town where we had arranged to meet. We stood there, slightly apart and repressed, as though we had just gone through a tragic event. The bus came up. We boarded it in silence.

'Where are we going? Where are you going to take me?' I broke the silence as we settled ourselves on the top deck.

'Somewhere,' he replied off-hand. 'Somewhere you often talked about. Somewhere you've often said you wanted to go. If it were anyone else, I should say I was gratifying a whim.' He smiled for the first time and looked at me. 'But I don't think you have anything so frivolous as whims, do you?' It was cold. I drew myself closer to him. 'An impossibility. You could only have obsessions.'

I wanted to be taken by the arm as he had done that first evening, and led blindly along without thinking or feeling anything, aware only of the arm tugging at mine, the solid ground under my feet, the feel of air in my face, and the place we were going to.

'I'll blindfold myself then shall I?' I asked, beginning to draw off my scarf. But Alasdair shrugged. 'A bit off,' he said, opening his paper. 'I'd rather you didn't. I should feel slightly uncomfortable and guilty that it was not the eye-hospital that I was taking my sick sister to.

All the same when the bus slid past the railway station and the rows of slate-roofed houses that led out of the town, I shut my eyes and allowed myself to be thrown gently to and fro between Alasdair and the side of the bus as we glided along. There was only the cold glass of the window, the side of his leg, the cigarette-smoke, the rustling newspaper and the coughing of the upper deck as we ran smoothly along. It was a gentle pleasure, being carried like that towards some unknown place.

It was a long ride, and we did not talk much. Alasdair sat still and silent behind his newspaper. Occasionally he read bits out with sardonic comments or with guffaws of laughter: the utterances of a peer or a film actress, the rise of the divorce rate, or the statistics of the soft-drink industry.

And then, abruptly, he slapped the newspaper under the seat and pushed us out of the bus, and we were standing alone at the side of the road, with the bus a green square on the horizon, loose gravel jumping under our feet as we walked, and the smell of tar and damp hedges.

Alasdair took out a map and studied it, running his finger along a line and pausing. I looked around. There were a few cottages here and there with ancient apple trees in the gardens, propped up with wooden stakes, an abandoned cart with 'Allington, Deerhurst' painted on the side, and beyond that, meadows running away into faint, low hills, and a mist covering everything.

Alasdair twisted round and thought hard for a moment and closed the map.

'Right,' he said. 'All set.' And we started walking across fields that were prickly with stubble. It stabbed round the sides of my shoes painfully, but soon there appeared a path, rutted deeply with cart-tracks and surrounded on either side by bushes of pale blackberries in tight bundles, and hedges littered with loose leaves and straw and twigs that the wind had blown there.

We walked briskly. Alasdair hummed a tune and scanned the horizon and took my arm. 'O.K.?' he smiled.

'Jolly good for the lungs this is. I haven't taken a proper walk for months. And soon I shall be back at the hospital and I shan't have a chance. London, whew!' he said; 'It's good, but it's best to carry an oxygen cylinder.'

'Shall I come to London when I am discharged?' I asked.

'Jolly good idea!' he laughed. 'You oughtn't to stick here at any rate! Look at that old Norman apse.'

Far away over the fields there were farm buildings, a patch of ground that had been half-ploughed and then abandoned, and a grey, crumbling church with a bell leaning from its tower.

We walked on. Except for the crackling of the stubble under our feet and the occasional squawk of a pheasant, there was silence. Even the birds seemed to have abandoned this strange, deserted stretch of country. There was nothing here but mild fields in the damp yellow of early autumn, and a far-away milky sky.

'I used to dream of living in a place like that, all alone with wide tracts of solitude all round, but now . . .'

'Your Wordsworthian serenity has been shattered,' he finished. 'Sorry!' he grimaced. 'Hungry yet?'

We walked and walked, Alasdair humming and breathing deeply and crying that it was good to be away from 'Dotheboys Hall' into some fresh air. We sat in a hedge to eat a pie and then walked again, until finally he stopped and peered behind and ahead and fumbled for his cigarettes.

He ran up a little hillock in the hedge, peered all round him and came down smiling.

'Well,' he asked, pointing behind us in the direction we had come from, 'how do you like it?'

I looked where he pointed. I looked all round. I could see that we had come a long way. And then as I stood, I recognized something. Far away behind us on the horizon was a hill; the hill that Judas Iscariot and I had waited upon for nearly a year. The same hill, except that we were on the other side.

'That is our hill, or rather *was* our hill . . . ' I began. But we were on the other side now, and between us and it the land was cut abruptly in half.

I ran across the stubble. I ran with pebble and mud crumbling into my shoes. Then I stopped, for it was as I had guessed. Below me, between us and the hill, was the darkest river I had ever seen. The world was broken in two by this heavy, dark grey river that stained its banks, and unfolded thickly beneath me like the slow thoughts of an old man.

It was not like the Thames, but wider and deeper and pulling strongly against its banks, fighting to be free. The banks were dark grey, and bordered with fine grey sand and powdered shell, and at the edges tough beds of white, vegetable-like celery shot up in stiff spikes towards the sky.

I had forgotten about Judas and the spy-glass, and the Green Hill, and the world on the other side. I had been taken there without even knowing it, and the other side

was a land not of dreams, but of things, solid things —
sand and rivers and coarse vegetable stuff, and Alasdair
leaning there against a hummock smoking and staring at
the horizon. The world of solid things. The world of
sanity. A sound woke me: the rustling of water as it
streamed over a log of wood that jutted out into the
river, and Alasdair's voice calling:

'Well, are you satisfied?'

'What is it called? And where does it go?'

'It's the Severn.'

I wanted to make a fire. I hoped the smoke would rise
high up into the sky and over the hill so that Judas could
see. I went and poked the celery. It was stiff and creaked.
I tugged up some grasses. Alasdair watched. He rolled
over on his back and blew smoke into the sky and
watched from there. A pale sun slid along behind the
veil of mist.

'Well?' he repeated. 'Are you pleased? Is this "strange
and dark and opposite" enough for you? What are you
doing over there?'

I had already built up a pile of grass and twigs and
long spikes of river growth. He stretched out his hand
and flicked on his lighter. The fire cracked up and a
sheet of flame spurted out. It roared for a moment and
then fell apart, dead.

Alasdair stretched out his lighter and tried again, still
lying on his back. The flames flickered and mounted for a
moment and then collapsed. 'Damp,' he said. He rose
slowly to his feet and sauntered across the field to the

hedge, and bent over, stooping along the ground silently and methodically, until his hands and arms were full and bulging with twigs and wood.

We packed the fire tightly together, stuffed in dead leaves, and laid piles of wood round it. The flames roared up and caught on the twigs, and the fire hissed and smoked and sent sheets of silvery vapour over us. Alasdair had found an old potato at the edge of a ploughed field. We laid it at the side in the hot cinders.

He lay back on his arms. 'Well? Are you pleased?' I nodded, and poked at the fire.

'You have to jump over it,' he murmured rolling on to his face and staring at the fire. 'It's a symbol of fertility or something, you know. You have to poke it,' he whispered drowsily, 'and a lot more besides.'

'I was just thinking . . .'

'You are always thinking.' He reached across the sinking flames and touched my nose. 'Just ash. You are always thinking, always preoccupied with grand cosmological things-as-a-whole. You're so existential. That's what I like about you.' He stretched out again and caught my ankle. 'Tell me about the man who tried to kiss you, the man who had teeth that jutted out and all that. Was it as bad as all that?'

'He was a research student in history. He had invited me to tea, and he was just talking about the problem of the Great Seal before King John's time, when suddenly he switched the wireless on and started squeezing me and pressing me. "Are we going to dance?" I asked, "because

I'm not very good at that kind of thing. At least, I can do an Eightsome, but there aren't enough of us for that." He was puffing and panting and it did not seem like the same man who had been talking about the Exchequer Rolls a moment before. I held my breath and counted ten hoping it would be over by that time, and to pass the time I tried to picture him in other disguises as well as that. I tried to picture him as a huntsman in a green velvet hat, and then in a bowler, and then I started to laugh and could not stop, and he seemed rather put out when I told him.'

'I am sure he was. Most men are very sensitive about their performance. Still, you managed to weather that one, you cool objective creature.'

'I don't think I am cool any more.'

'No. Perhaps not. What will you do when you leave here?'

I could hear the whisper of water behind us; the tiny waterfall rolling over the log into the river. The fire smoked. The future was there, all round us.

'The future,' I embraced it with my arms, 'on this side of the hill. Here.'

'That's right,' Alasdair whispered. 'The future's nothing to be afraid of.' He rolled over the fire to my side and slid his arms underneath me.

The smoke from the fire fluttered and faded and merged in the pale sky. A pheasant squawked in a wood. I prodded the potato. It was soft. I picked it out lovingly, broke it in half, and gave half to Alasdair. I took a bite and was amazed at the grand gesture I had made. I had never made a gesture like that before, breaking food in half and handing half to a man to share. It was a grand, worldly gesture. The potato rested in my palm.

Alasdair took a bite of his and chucked it out towards the river. 'So much for Farmer Tingewick's potatoes.' He snatched my half and threw it in the other direction. 'We'll go to "The Bull" when we get back, so there is no need to stuff yourself with vegetable.'

He was close beside me, breathing heavily, with his hands on my wrists. I could feel his leg running down mine, and his face hovering over me. The draught from his nostrils tickled my face; his lips twitched like butterflies.

'You are so real,' he whispered. 'I'm afraid of the other ones, the people who possess the earth.'

He stretched farther over and pushed his face closer until I could only see the whites of his eyes, and hear his breathing, heavy and close, and feel hot sheets of air pouring down my throat.

The feel of solid things is very good; the feel of the hard sand by the river; the feel of the stone wall of the settlement, the feel of water when you are thirsty, the cold of a glass after a nightmare, and the sound of another voice that is not your own talking.

The water flowed noisily over the jutting-out wood; the fire fell to powder in its hearth, and we lay there.

'No one was unkind at Oxford,' I said softly, dreamily, almost to myself. 'They were very friendly as they passed, it was just that I did not have the knack of existing.'

I was gazing at my past. I was clutching at Alasdair as though it were a matter of life and death, as though my salvation lay in holding on there.

'You exist for me, at any rate,' he whispered urgently. 'Too much so in fact! Come on, nice thing. Come on, let's get ready.'

He was moving slowly about, stooping over with his back to me, fumbling with his jacket, patting his pockets, and untying his shoe-laces.

As he stooped or stood erect, bent or fumbled, the world seemed to close in till it was like a room with walls and ceilings. It was because of that that I obeyed the summons to share what reality there was with someone else. It put a floor under your feet, and even though it was odd, inappropriate; even though it was painful, that seemed part of the mysterious instructions to use any means you have to cling to that which is real because it may establish something further.

I felt nothing more, though, only the discomfort of this initiation ceremony and his heavy breathing and clutching, for life or death. At last Alasdair was lying on his side apart and breathing deeply and peacefully. I felt slightly sick, and the hill and everything seemed a long way away. Even Alasdair seemed distant.

He got up after a bit and wiped his face and went down to the river and stooped over the dark grey and drank. He came back wiping himself and smiling.

'All right?' he asked. It seemed as though he were calling over a distance. 'It's always a bit odd the first time.'

I nodded numbly.

'A matter of adjustment,' he went on, 'like a new screw that's stiff, if you'll excuse the delicate metaphor.' He smiled contentedly, and licked the river water from round his mouth. 'Just a matter of adjustment.' He looked sleek and satisfied like a cat.

'You mean next time we come here . . . ?'

He was bending over his shoe-laces. Perhaps he did not hear. I could see him smiling as he put himself together.

It was a new and strange experience to me, and it did not surprise me that I did not enjoy it. I had not expected pleasure, only some contact with the real world, and that I had found. Only my head felt odd, as though it were not mine, and the world seemed farther, not nearer.

Alasdair saw me leaning on my shoulder staring down at the river. He caught my hand and lay back staring at the wide sky.

'Hungry?' he asked.

'Now that we are . . . are lovers,' I supposed that was the word, '. . . will we come here often and light a fire and cook and eat? We could make a kind of camp here.' Strange music was running in my head. 'We could make a kind of retreat from the settlement. You said you hated it there.'

'Hey! Ho!' he carolled. 'Hey ho the holly, this life is so jolly.'

We left the river without saying good-bye – I thought we should return there tomorrow or the day after or at the week-end, every week-end – and Alasdair talked and laughed all the way back to the road. When we got to where the bus had dropped us, the first lorry that he thumbed stopped. We climbed up into the high cabin, and Alasdair and the driver started talking about the new motorway, and generally exchanging motorists' experiences till we arrived back at the town.

The lorry left us at the railway yard, and as we got down I saw the driver wink and twist up the corner of his mouth knowingly.

'I suppose now that we are lovers,' I began when we were alone, 'there are many things to talk about.'

He sighed and smiled and touched my nose. 'Words! You funny thing! Words! Verbigeration! You know you will spoil everything if you have to verbalize about it. Words never work properly. Life is difficult, subtle, complex. Life, as Lawrence might say, is a "winged gift". Words are always inadequate to express the complexity of a situation.'

He paused and looked at me and frowned. 'You are not afraid of the future are you? With your cool, objective, detached view of everything, you shouldn't be. How I envy you! The trouble with me is that I get too worked up about things, and then afterwards I commit myself in ways that I don't really intend and get myself into a lot of bother. How are you feeling now? Hungry?'

'Not really. The other is more important.'

'What other?' He frowned again and his voice had a sharp edge. I had never noticed it before and I was slightly afraid. I suddenly felt isolated and alone.

'What other?' he repeated impatiently.

'Our life together,' I fumbled clumsily. 'You have initiated me into a new life.' The words sounded silly. 'No one has ever loved me before,' I added. 'Perhaps that was why I got caught in the fowler's snare.'

'Unworldly little Josephine.' His voice softened and I was relieved. I was afraid to open the subject again. 'Let's go into "The Bull" and have a drink and some food before the place-up-on-the-top-of-the-hill closes.'

'The Bull' was dark and quiet except for a few old men shuffling round the dart-board, and some younger ones sitting on tall stools by the bar, who turned round as we came in and turned back perfunctorily.

We went to a table in the corner, and Alasdair bought a pint and a half of bitter and some pies, and bit his teeth in.

My mouth was dry. I felt numbed and confused, and afraid of stumbling into something that was wrong.

'Not hungry?' he asked.

He ate alone and in silence. When he had finished he picked up his tankard and smiled at me. 'We had a nice afternoon didn't we? Are you pleased that I found that river for you, and took you to the other side of your hill?'

I nodded mechanically.

'Bless you!' He wiped his mouth and swilled the last

remains of his beer round the glass. 'I feel strong enough to beard the day-room and the Doctor's rounds again tomorrow.'

'You told me once,' I ventured timidly, 'that you had no success with women.'

'Well?' he waited, unhelpful, fiddling with his watch-strap.

'Have I helped?'

'Of course!' he sighed. 'My own life has no depths, no subtlety, no hidden parts. That's why I've enjoyed going out with you today. I wish we had more time though. You remind me that another world exists, and that's so refreshing, isn't it?'

'You aren't, you weren't . . . suffering from schizo-phrenia then?' I blurted out.

He exploded with laughter. 'Good heavens, no!' Then he stopped sharply. 'Sorry,' he choked, 'sorry I can't oblige you there.'

'Oh, I'm sorry then. I suppose I misunderstood you in the board-room, that first night. I'm sorry. I hope . . . I hope I haven't insulted you.'

'Not at all,' he assured me. 'On the contrary, I'm flattered that you should find those mysterious terrains of the imagination in me.'

He grinned and grimaced in his old way. 'Nice after-noon it's been. Very good for me, and for you too, I hope. Knocked a few of the old corners off, hasn't it? Shall we run and try to catch that bus?'

'Shall we see each other tomorrow as usual?' I asked

anxiously as we stood in the entrance hall saying good night.

'Right you are. Tomorrow evening as ever was,' Alasdair repeated gaily, bending over and kissing me lightly on the cheek, a gentle brush. 'Nice girl. Nice Josephine. Nice day.'

I felt my way blindly up the corridor. The night nurse was bending over the report-book in the office. She only twisted her head round as I passed and grinned and said:

'Been gallivanting? That's right. Makes a change.'

I crept into bed in the darkness.

Almost at once the light clicked on; the Sister was standing there. I had not seen her for a week, not since the evening in the clinical room when she had snapped a mask over her face and wheeled the shrieking trolley down to the dormitory. She stood there on the bare boarding in the middle of the floor, with the laundry-book in her hand. It was too late for her, I thought, she should have gone off duty three hours ago.

'Dearie,' she stood there, taking in everything as though it were for the first time. The light shone fiercely on the bare boarding, and I noticed the cracks between each board, and followed each one, uneasily, obsession-ally, till it ran into the wall.

She stood there not smiling. Her lips were slightly apart, her eyes careful and observant. Her hands clasped the note-book tightly.

'Has your life become so full since the party that you

cannot be in bed . . . ?' she started to smile and stopped.
'It is good that you should spend your life outside here
now; but where do you go? I waited till eight last night
and the night before, and then the night nurses told me
you did not come in until eleven.' Her voice dropped in
agitation. 'Where do you go?'

I shook my head. I was still numb and confused.

'If it is with your new friends, I am only glad that you
have found a niche at last. That is an entirely good thing,
for tomorrow the committee is meeting and you will be
regraded. It is only a formality as I have told you before,
and they may not even wish to see you. But you must
ask Mrs. Maybury for the afternoon off just in case. And
so . . . ' her eyelids trembled and she stretched her arms
out towards me, 'and so, my dear, I am glad. This little
incident in your life will be closed, and you will fly away,
as we said before, into the busy world again, from under
the leaves. Do you think you will find a quiet, really
sympathetic, thoughtful young woman to share a flat
with? Or a hostel perhaps . . . '

'Or why not,' I interrupted dreamily, 'a husband?'

The Sister made no immediate reaction. She only
smiled faintly and said in a long-drawn-out, meditative,
voice, at least pretending to agree, 'Yes, of course!
Marriage is important. But not just yet. I do not think of
your marrying just yet. You must remember that you
have been ill and what you need after a severe trial like
that is a bannister. A strong bannister that is not rooted
in, shall we say, fleeting emotions. It is always good to

have such a bannister. My father was one to me, a very firm one, and when he died I found I was no longer in need of such a support. So dearie, stay round the hospital tomorrow. I think when your status is changed you will feel a good bit better and more settled about the future.'

I buried my face in the pillow and laughed bitterly.

'What is it? May we share it or am I too slow for these English jokes?' She touched my shoulder timidly. 'What is it dearie, what is it?'

'Do you think I care about my status?' I whispered. 'Do you think I care whether I am ever regraded or not? Do you think I care whether the Doctors and hospital board decide I am sane or insane? I don't care tuppence about nice quiet friends. Mine is not going to be that kind of existence. I want to live, to feel. I was born for something more than mere sanity. I was born for so much joy. A great possibility of joy. More than you could ever imagine. My life is far different than you could imagine,' I was shouting.

She paused, biting her lip. She blinked and stared at the shutters, and then said quietly:

'It is his fault mostly.' She was talking chiefly to herself. She was talking bitterly. 'It is his fault mostly; he should not have allowed you to misunderstand. You are innocent. You live in a world of your own, and he has abused this good life.' She choked. 'I have seen you when you were ill. I care what happens and I was greatly disturbed when the night nurses told me. For you know, indivisible people are not easily divided, at least, not without great pain. You live in a world of your own, and he has abused this innocence.'

'A world of my own?' I broke out at last, enraged. 'Do you think I am not a real person? Do you think I don't have feelings and passions as real as anyone? You try to *keep* me in a world of my own! You treat me like a mental invalid. You cherish me like a diseased person. Why not put a coloured ribbon in my hair and make me wear flowered pinafores, as they do on the chronic wards? But I am real. I was born for joy, for so much joy, for love . . . ' But I suppose I doubted it really, for I wept.

She nodded sadly. 'Tell me,' she picked up my hand. 'Tell me all about him.' She held it between hers and pressed it, 'Tell me all about him.'

I drew it away. 'Tell me then,' she repeated timidly. 'I am sorry if I treat you like an invalid. I do not regard you so; far from it. But I have seen you ill and well, and I care. Tell me,' she whispered gently, 'tell me.' But I was silent. 'Tell me.'

I stared at her for a long time. 'Excuse me,' I said at last, 'but there is a crumb on your top lip, one that has got left behind in the general march downstairs. It may be the same one as last week; observation confirms however, that it is not. It is slightly larger, in fact.'

She stood there dully, neutrally, for a moment, as though I had insulted her race, with her hands that should have clasped my hands, cupping nothing. Then she slowly drew out a handkerchief and humbly wiped round her mouth.

'Better?' she asked putting on a brighter smile. 'Good night dearie.'

She turned and left the room with swift, stilted steps like a doll, 'click-clock-click-clock' into the darkness, and then I caught sight of the heart-shaped gingerbread that she must have slipped furtively against the mirror when I was not looking or before I came in. I remembered her father who was her bannister, and the non-Aryan laws, and her deep suffering face, and I cried and cried. It did not seem only that afternoon that we had walked so happily through the stubble towards the River Severn. Everything was confused and blurred and uncertain. But it will be all right, I told myself at last, tomorrow when I have seen Alasdair. I will go and find him in the afternoon as soon as I get back.

Chapter Seven

I HAD a dream that night that left me limp and shaken. I thought I was condemned to death and was being taken by some monks to a church to be prepared.

They took my pulse and gave me syrup, and dressed me in a long white buttoned robe and showed me breathing exercises 'that would help to take the emotional strain'. And then I caught sight of the coffin, small and stocky, almost square, and the monks chuckling and remarking that I would have to bend double to get in. And then I was with Mother, revisiting our home; suddenly a child again, walking on a bright green grass verge. It **was** so bright that I was dazzled.

I screamed out and saw I was dreaming, and struggled for the light-switch. I staggered across the room to it, but when I got there it seemed to be wrapped in a jacket, like a shroud only soft, and I could not find its shape and switch it on.

I screamed again and then the light was on and the night nurse was standing there, her plump, soft hand enclosing the switch.

'There, there, it's all over now,' she grinned just as she had grinned last evening in the office. 'Just a dream! What is it then? Only a dream.'

It seemed that something horrible had gazed at me, and was still gazing. 'A gaze,' I whispered, thinking of death and the coffin and the bright green grass. 'A bad gaze.'

'A bad dream,' she corrected me reassuringly. 'It's all over now. You are awake.' She was short and plump and kind. 'Everything's all right,' she repeated firmly, taking hold of my shoulder, and leading me towards the bed. 'A dream, that's all.'

I could not go back to bed. It was like the coffin.

'That's simple,' she chuckled, and dragged the chair over to the bed. 'I'll sit here for a bit.'

I could not get in though, so I sat in the chair and she sat on the bed opposite, our knees touching, and she broke the sandwich she had been eating in two and gave me half. She sat there, smiling and winking and munching, her heavy jaw champing up and down over the meat and raw onion, as she talked about her family, her home, and how happy they were. The cosiest family in 'Wartons', she said; 'only had the telly on when the kids were safe in bed, and went to the sea every other summer.'

I tried to listen, but I could only think of my childhood

and Mother, and death and the bright green. 'Yes,' I
mumbled mechanically, 'Oh yes. How nice.'

'At Southend, you know,' she tried to catch my eye
and my attention, 'do you know, you won't believe
it...'

I tried to believe it. But the dream gazed at me again.
I shook my head.

'Go on,' she urged. 'Guess what? Guess what?' She
breathed onion over me and her round face broke into a
grin like the monks'. 'You've got to guess!'

'I can't,' I croaked. I was still shivering.

'Well you must *try*,' she winked. 'I'll give you three
guesses.' Her knees were pressing hard against mine
now. The onion and the smile were overpowering. I
tried to concentrate on what she was wanting me to do.
'Three guesses. Well come on! Snap out of it!' she
nudged. 'What is there at the seaside? What is there at
the sea? Let's have it,' she jollied me.

Sitting opposite the bed, I tried to guess. My feet
were cold. 'Well, there's the sea,' I began hopelessly. I
wanted Alasdair. 'I can't guess. You must tell me.
Sometimes there are caravans along the beach, and birds
above, I suppose.'

'Well,' she began triumphantly and loudly as though
she were whipping out a prize-card. 'Shall I tell you?
Slot-machines, of course! All along the front ... *Fish
and chips out of a slot-machine!* Hot too, and a knife
and fork,' she chuckled. She leaned back, her arms
folded in satisfaction. 'How's that? Fish and chips out

of a slot-machine, and a tiny cardboard knife and fork.'

Then her face fell. I was still sitting there shivering and clutching for something else and she was suddenly sorry that she had failed. 'Do you like budgies?' she asked, turning away subdued.

She went away and came back in a few moments with a bottle and a glass and measured something into water and gave it to me to drink. In the half-light of the early morning I could see that it glittered and shivered. It was paraldehyde. I had not tasted that for months. Not since before the start of the long, hot summer.

I drank it eagerly though, and it swept over me and carried me rapidly away like a river, while she sat there with her fat knees pressed against the bed, turning the pages of a magazine and eating.

I woke up feeling drugged and sick and stupid, and they brought me breakfast in bed because of the 'bad gaze' in the night. When I had eaten some I fell asleep again and only woke up when it was past midday, and the light was sucking the closed curtains in and out and in, and cheerful voices were coming from the tennis courts. The dream still hung over me in a cloud.

I got dressed quickly because I wanted to find Alasdair. We had not arranged where and when, but it seemed natural that he should be somewhere, either at the ha-ha or by the tennis courts. I thought this meeting would erase the night and the dream and my sudden depression. I thought Alasdair would even laugh and explain it all in a rational way, and that the glass-cover that was over me would break. I needed him badly, I thought.

He was not in the ha-ha or by the tennis courts. I walked up and down the drive and across to the O.T. huts, but he was not there either. I even crept cautiously up to the board-room, but there were voices coming from inside, and a cardboard notice on the door said: 'Engaged! Do not enter.'

I went slowly across the drive to the male side, thinking perhaps he was up in his room, or had gone out. I could see them there in the bow-window moving backwards and forwards like shadows. I called in, but the male nurse looked out, so I went round to the other side, and called again: 'Where is Alasdair, is he there?'

The schizophrenic boy was sitting under the table with red plastic scissors in his hand, slashing rhythmically at an enormous paper butterfly made from the *Sunday Graphic*. He edged over to the window and stared at me dully. Then in a kind of panic he withdrew to the table, his eyes narrowing and his fair hair falling over his face.

'Please,' I implored, 'come back, and speak a bit louder so that I can hear what you are saying. Where is Alasdair? Is he in there?'

He shook his head blankly.

'Where is he then? Is he in his room? Will you go and find him and tell him it's me, Josephine?'

He shook his head again and frowned and I was afraid. He looked so tormented.

'Where is he then? Is he ill?' I demanded. 'It's rather urgent.'

The boy stuck his arm blindly and protectively round his face, and ran away, his head still buried in his elbow.

'I get browned off,' he muttered. 'Voices, voices, always voices. I get cheesed off.' I could hear him stampeding down the corridor, and I was sad that I had upset him.

'Do you know where Alasdair is?' I called to the old man in the black beret who sat near the window. I knew him so well from across the drive. I could see now that it was a Bible that he clutched. It was full of narrow strips of paper that he was still inserting as I talked. 'Is he in his room do you think?'

The old man carefully tore another strip and inserted it. The Bible bulged at the spine, it was so full of reference strips. 'Who?' he asked.

'Alasdair Faber. The one with fair hair who is always laughing and talking.'

He chuckled. 'You mustn't ask me questions like that. They've been giving me the treatment for years now, "maintenance", and I don't remember anything.' He giggled. 'I lose everything overnight. That is why I am here. I have to begin again afresh each day. Every day is the *First* Day to me, the day when God created Adam,' and he laughed again. 'That's the electric done that for me.'

There were still the red marks round his temples

where the apparatus had been applied. An instinct made me move away.

'Maintenance ECT,' he was still explaining cheerfully as I crossed the drive, 'that's what put paid to my memory.'

When I got back to the ward it was in a state of chaos. The older women were taking off their coloured pinafores. The younger ones were making themselves up. Some of them were running round with dusters. Others were putting saucers under the cups at the tea tables, and laying piles of pale crumpets beside the gas-stove to be toasted, and cutting packs of green ice-cream into cubes and laying them in saucers. Of course, the committee was coming round.

'All right, Josephine?' the Sister called as I passed the office. 'The bad dream vanquished? Don't wander too far though just in case the committee wants to see you in person. Just a formality, but a worth-while one. Yes?'

She paused and smiled at me as though she had forgotten last night. Then she stared hard. 'You must eat a big tea,' she said gently. 'That will clear your head. But first,' she was handing me a feather duster, 'do the tops of the pictures for me, dearie.'

But I went back across the drive, beyond the bay-window to the other side of the men's day-room. This time it was the other child I saw; the epileptic.

'Where is Alasdair?' I called in.

He was sitting by the table on the floor clutching a child's red wool dress. His hand was a bird fluttering in and out. The dress was a house, the sleeve was a stair, and the hem was the saloon where the bird sat.

'Do you know where Alasdair is?' I repeated. But the male nurse was there standing beside the boy.

'Wanting anyone?' he asked insolently, stepping between us.

'I'm looking . . .'

'If you're looking for Mr. Faber,' he sniggered, 'he's gone. Bad luck, but he's gone! He was off this morning without even his seventy-two hours' notice.'

'Are you sure you mean Alasdair Faber?'

He nodded and took a step back because I smelt of paraldehyde. 'He was ready for discharge in any case. Getting too active.' The statutory four inches at the bottom of the window came down with a slam.

I leaned against the wall and thought. The feather duster was still there beside me. He had left without telling me, he had suddenly gone, taking with him just what I was looking for. Everything seemed a long way off. He seemed to have taken everything with him, and the gardens had become stiff and straight and flat like a canvas. The geraniums were too bright. They had been painted in badly.

I leaned against the wall and looked in to the room and watched the bird. It drew honey from the buttons which were its cups. I just stood there for a long time watching the bird. It was suddenly peaceful.

At last I turned back towards the ward. My feet were a hair's breadth off the ground, and everything was light like paper. The receptionist smiled at me as I passed her box.

'Good day,' she said daintily.

I grinned foolishly. 'Good day,' I replied, raising an imaginary hat.

I could see them down the ward, like through the bad end of a telescope. Or rather I could see their feet ticking over the polished floors and their mouths opening and shutting in the dining-room, and the crumpets going up and down, up and down, in long rows. I supposed they must be eating their tea. I laughed and doffed my hat again.

I went to my room. I thought I would get out my map of the Thames and Severn Canal and follow it up till it came to the Severn. It flopped open beside me on to the bed, and as I lay there I heard faint music and saw that Alasdair was in the window opposite. Only he was in disguise. He had put on fancy-dress, and was playing the mouth-organ, jigging up and down in the upstairs room, winking and whistling and playing the mouth-organ in a flashy tie. I drew the curtain to shut it out, and started to follow the Thames and Severn Canal the way I loved.

There was a tap at the door. The receptionist stood there with the same smile still on her face. She told me how Alasdair had had to 'push off'. She handed me a letter, and some flowers. 'With his love,' she said carefully.

I bit one of the flower-heads off and chewed it. I

giggled. She smiled faintly and disappeared. The flowers and the letter fell to the floor. The mouth-organ still came from the room where Alasdair had been, and I supposed the man was still grimacing out across the lawns, but I did not mind now. I lay back on the bed and thought of the smoke rising up from the fire we had made on the other side of the hill, and the potato I had divided in two and shared, and the sound of the running water. That was the first friendship I had ever made. Perhaps it was the last, or perhaps it had been an illusion throughout; had just been for Alasdair the only way of passing an unusually boring summer.

But there *was* a form of contact. I could not deny that. Something had changed in me, and I could not neglect it any more than I could deny having been to the other side of the hill.

My eye followed the canal past Sapperton, under the hill, till it emerged in the Golden Valley. But my mind was reaching out ahead for the place where it joined the River Severn. The Severn had come between me and my past. It was irrevocable.

Something drew me to my feet; urged me up, propelled me towards the door and downstairs. It was the need to keep alive, the need to hold on to what little reality there was, to keep within the ring that was people, even though they were not the ones that peopled the big houses of North Oxford.

The Sister, I could see as I went down the drive, was at the window calling to me to stop, putting her mouth to the four-inch gap at the bottom and crying and waving her hands.

'Josephine, dearie,' her voice floated out urgently. 'You are wanted now. They want to see you now, so quickly! quick!'

But when I heard her I only ran. I did not mind what grade I was given in society, or whether I made the grade at all. I only wanted to keep alive. So I ran and ran, faster and faster, down the drive, out into the main road, and down the hill that led to the town. The pavement seemed to come up to meet me and then to be far away. Up and down, up and down it jerked, and the cars appeared suddenly out of nothing, and I could not tell where they were or how far away. I stood still in fright. A car drew up beside me.

'Can I take you anywhere?' a cultured voice drawled. I shook my head and waited.

'Cheer up,' another man called. 'Hasn't he turned up? Never mind Better luck next time.'

Then I found that I must at last have learned a rule.

''Sright,' I found myself replying to him in a strange idiom that was not mine, with a fatuous smile that was not mine. I started to walk briskly. I thought only of getting to the town.

I passed the railway yard and the bus station, and then I came to 'The Bull' where Alasdair and I had been the evening before. It was just opening time when I swung the door open and went up to the counter and climbed on to a high stool.

'Hallo, hallo,' said the man I sat next to in surprise.

'Hallo, hallo,' I replied.

'And what is it you'll have?' he asked after a pause, while I got my breath.

'Half of bitter, please.'

But bitter it turned out was not 'a lady's drink', so he made it gin, and I drank and drank, and late that night we found a hotel where the landlady welcomed us pleasantly. I had not brought my pyjamas and tooth-brush and things, but that did not seem to matter. It was worth anything to catch what little there was of existence and cling to it.

Chapter Eight

IT WAS a hollowness in the head and arms and legs that drew me on and on, down country lanes where leaves flickered, in and out of the bare, harvested fields, towards the noise of main roads, and away from it. It was a lightness that drove me on, as if I might be blown away altogether or fly off and up like a piece of paper in the wind, unless I found one feature under which I existed. It was this that drove me across the paths, under the heavy, creaking trees and on to the arterial roads.

Sometimes as I was walking cars purred softly up in felted smoothness and men with cool velvet accents offered me lifts and cigarettes and then suggested drinks at roadhouses as we sped towards the roaring trunk roads. I thought I wanted nothing more than that, an assurance as we sped forwards that I was alive, that I was not flying through unpeopled regions and grey wastes of space, never again to be touched or crossed at any point.

Sometimes as I crossed the by-passes on foot a man would lean down from the cabin of his lorry and bawl:

'Cheer up! It's not as bad as all that!' as he ground by, although I was not miserable at all, only feather-weight. Or sometimes the lorry would pull up and wait, and the driver would lean out letting his ash flutter down till I was abreast, then:

'Where do you want to be going?' he would murmur.

It did not matter where. I would tell him that, climbing up beside him. 'It was of no consequence at all.'

And so a kind of pattern was established. When I said it did not matter, he would say: ''sright', and hand me a 'Weights' which would lie crumpled and crushed in my hands. And when he continued:

'It's getting nippy these mornings,' I would reply: ''Sright.'

It was all so simple. Perhaps this was how things were done, how Rome was built. It did not happen in a day, as Mother had been fond of reminding me.

I had travelled a long way like this; from lorry to car, from trunk-road to lane, on the by-pass or sitting alone in the hedges, and I had lost count of the time or the number of days that I had been walking.

I had been travelling with a man who said he was a 'representative', was well known in these parts, and that a little farther on there was the 'Beaton Arms' where there was trout, partridge or caviare, or something of worth – I forget what it was. Perhaps I would like to go there, he suggested, and have a blow-out or something, and since we hit it off so well together . . .

'You get me? Just the devil in me,' he winked. We laughed together. It all seemed to be part of the game that kept the lightness away.

But the next day he had got up early when I was barely awake, and left abruptly saying he was rather *too* well known in these parts, and that if his wife got the wind up he might get into hot water. He told me, however, that he would be there at the same time next week on his rounds, and what about it? I agreed except that there was the money which I told him that I did not have, and he winked and tossed me several notes. We made our rendezvous, and he went off whistling.

I was sorry when his car disappeared round the bend and I was alone again. For he did not seem to mind about anything. He did not seem to mind about your not saying the right things or being a proper kind of person who knew about getting into 'hot water', or talked much or laughed in the right places. He seemed to think ''sright' was all right as we swerved down country lanes, across wide commons and through to the towns.

It was just the comfort of sitting beside him there like a sheep huddling against a wall at night and shutting out the bare tracts and empty places that were all round. It was just that that recurred as I watched his car disappearing. The hollowness had come back and I hoped someone else would turn up before very long.

I was on a railway bridge then, I remember, a junction I think, because trains were shunting backwards and forwards, and there were yards on one side. On the other was a churchyard with tombstones bearing messages and blackbirds resting on the top-sides, sharpening their beaks. I just stood while the steam floated up from the shifting trains, and thought of the messages of the dead underground and the blackbirds on top. I must, I suppose, have stood there for a long time, because a man who had been loitering in the background making little nibbling noises with his teeth, came up, glancing round and asking me if I knew what time it was. I could not suggest any time that it might be, and I wondered if he had come to take away the lightness and nothing that were floating over again.

Seeing that I did not know the time, he asked me if he could trouble me for a match, and pointed out that it was cold and draughty standing on the bridge and suggested that we should go round the back-doubles to the 'Whistle'.

I was just trying to decide whether it would be a good thing to make my way with him or not – it was one of Mother's maxims never to look a gift-horse in the mouth – when he started making little nibbling noises again with his lips, and I ran away. The man started to follow then he turned and drifted in the other direction and I was left alone on the bridge.

Someone in a mackintosh with a rosette came up. It was a non-male smiling at me.

'Under the weather?' she asked briskly and challengingly. 'May I help?' She pointed to the rosette. It was the kind that football supporters wear, only in the middle of it it said: 'Strike a goal for Jesus.' She was telling me that the actual present world was a very different kettle of fish from the one God planned. 'Man as God planned him,' she started to explain to me. 'Imagine starting to build yourself a new house, and every time the workmen . . . ' She smelt of cotton cloth, the kind you get in long bales, and there was a speck of cabbage gleaming on her tooth.

'I'm not in unpleasure at all,' I assured her. She began to contradict me, telling me urgently about how the blue-prints had been, and as she leaned forward I could see the man standing on the corner of the bridge, smoking and shuffling and looking towards us and away.

The blue-prints. The metal bridge was rusty, with spotted newspaper, and paper-bags stamped with messages, rustling at the edges, and there was the churchyard, the coke-works and miles of stained gravel railway track stretching away to nothing. The wagons rolled backwards and forwards beneath; wisps of steam formed and dissolved round my legs, and the messages cried all round: 'Christ is all,' or 'Pannels for Superity Footwear'.

There was nothing but a blank, and a non-male in a mackintosh with a flapping rosette and a mouth open inquiringly. It was just then that the policeman came up and asked me if I were 'Miss Josephine Traughton'.

I giggled, it sounded so funny. So inexact, and so improbable in this haze of gravel and smoke and sidings. It was such a second-rate accusation, I thought, that it hardly rang true.

I shook my head. 'I never was that name,' I told him emphatically. 'Though I once tried to be. It was not a success though.'

He was asking me about my abode, but as the gentleman I was primarily with was not here till next week, I could not tell him what my proposed address was either, or where I planned to spend the night.

'In any case,' I assured him, 'it is of no consequence because whatsoever it may turn out to be, I shall only be here for a few days. You see I make a point of keeping fairly loose in my habitat – on the move most of the time, shall we say.'

The policeman was looking through his note-book, hardly attending to the gist of my argument, and asking me to go along with him to the station for a check-up. I pointed out to him that I had a prior engagement, two in fact, and anyhow that name and address had never been more than a very rough and ready approximation to the truth. Many things had happened to change the course of my life since the days when they were established. These data were therefore anachronisms and could hardly be said to hold.

They seemed, however, very anxious that I should step into their car and go with them to the station, even though I pointed out that the man I was primarily with would be waiting for me next week (and I did not like letting people down), and also that there was very little that I wanted, apart from keeping the lightness out (though I assured them how much I appreciated the service and their putting their most comfortable car at my disposal). Finally, however, I thought it might be just as well if I went with them as with him. Who knows?

The scientist was standing beside my bed and I was complaining:

'It was an unmeasured and unthoughtful act though. You see, they brought me back here, and when the Scottish dancing starts up, and the hearse went down the drive containing someone who was no longer *en vie*, I tried to run out, back to the lanes, and each time the black box came crashing down round my head. It was unthoughtful,' I complained, 'because I want so little of life. I assure you, there's nothing I want to be cured of. I only want to be left to wander freely and independently of any rules.'

I was standing at the window as usual waiting for my friend when the scientist came up and stood beside me. They used to do that often, asking me primarily why I remained silent and would not talk to them. It was funny that they could not see this, namely that besides its not being necessary in the slightest, there was nothing actually that I wanted to say. So I began to get a bit tired of all the questionnaires that were being put out, and the sessions of guessing games which they seemed to be more versed in than I. There were questions about my thoughts and my health and my way of life. For their statistics and bulletins, I supposed. Once I heard them say something about consciousness – or was it constipation? – at any rate they thought I had a high degree of it, which meant that there was a great psychic opportunity, which I was glad to hear of. 'But frankly, though I am quite willing to co-operate in any research – indeed, I once nearly became a philological researcher myself – I do not see much point in their picking on me.' So I tell the scientists politely that they must try someone else, and that if their agent must stand there, could she stand just a little farther to the right as she was interfering with my view.

'You see, down the sides of the quarters where I am stationed there are long windows, though to get a proper view you have to prise the beds apart, and sometimes in the moil a locker or two gets spilled, which is unfortunate but not really when you think of it.

'How time flies, sir! What a long time you have been sitting beside me! What a long conference, what a long confabulation! If you propose to stay, sir, would you mind just shifting your chair a little farther to the right as you affect my view, and I am anxious not to miss my friend. Ah, but I see you are going. "Quite so, you must be making tracks." Perhaps then you would be kind enough to remember your little promise about fetching me my clothes and a key for I must be off. I have a rendezvous as I told you, and I don't like letting people down; it's not in my practice.

'And while we are on it, I might as well let you know that I prefer to go around without the police who so kindly asked me if I were all right and feeling fit, and thoughtfully escorted me here. As a matter of fact I *was* all right. So you see there was no need for them to worry. Perhaps you would do me the kindness to tell them that? Though it was kind of them to take all that trouble, I prefer to be alone. Thank you, thank you. Good-bye.

'By the way, one moment, if by any chance my friend should wish to find me, I forget his name, sir, you could tell him the room where I am to be located is a very large one and there are beds ranged all along the walls, side by side, end to end, some found to have occupants during the light hours, others not. I decided long ago, on former visits, that the station must be for statistics or drug-research, so I christened it the Settlement.

'But they say it is not for either of these two purposes, and not to bother my head about things like that, though I am sure M. would have been anxious to know who made up my little circle of cronies. But I recall they say that it is discourteous to call one's Mother M. even though she is dead. All the laboratory assistants seem to agree on this point. So I noted it down in the book of rules that I am compiling for those who follow – N.B. that it is rude to call one's Mother M. even though she is dead.

'I had to have a little chuckle after I had inscribed it, for you see, now I had collected eighteen rules, some to do with one's family and their representatives, others to do with one's little social world. The rules of what to do and what to say in order to be authentic. When I had twenty I considered this would be sufficient to set me on the road.

'In the next bed is Judas Iscariot. I did not know that women could be called by this name too. Sometimes the scientists and the laboratory technicians shut her in a cupboard. I used to think that this might be for jam-making sessions, as Mrs. Iscariot is known to be a house-wife. But they say that this is not so either, so now I do not know. In fact I do not know anything; so I do not bother to say anything any more.

'I used to once, mark you! When I was at school and at the University I used to say quite a lot of things, quite often too. But they always turned out to be wrong, they were never the correct ones. Consequently the output grew poorer and poorer until finally they caught me out at Waterminster Place; that was at the party. So now I stay silent. It is better that way, though the technicians say that it is rude not to speak to your friends and representatives when they come to see you on visiting days.

'Actually I have told them that I do not require them to come and sit there any more visiting me. For one thing, it means turning my chair round in the other direction away from the window and having my view of the hill interrupted.

'For another, I have a rendezvous that it would be

highly discourteous not to keep. So you see, I must be off! Up the hill, and down on to the other side where the river is. The car will come up the hill and the owner will stop just a little way ahead, and open the window and light up and sit there smoking until I come abreast. It is all very simple, modest and unexalted, and I should be glad if the police did not keep bothering me. It was kind of them to be so solicitous, but on the whole I prefer to be left to make my own way through life. And perhaps at the same time you would be so kind as to bring me my clothes and unlock the door at the end of the establishment. You see, they keep it locked, I gather, lest any "undesirables" should gain access. But to recapitulate, strictly speaking, I should be off by now. I have a rendezvous at the "Beaton Arms" for soon after six, which strictly speaking, if you see what I mean, I should not rescind, especially as I owe a small sum of money. So it is high time that I was gone. But why do you converge on me instead of separating out? I assure you there is nothing I wish to be cured of. No, indeed, nothing! Have I not succeeded at last in acquiring the rules of the game? Maybe my play is a little surprising but it works as well as Helena and Prue and Sally's. So take those needles away and that rubber gag and the black box, for it is high time that I was gone ...'

For a long time it seemed to go on like this, the endless colloquys with the doctors and nurses, and then the attempts to free myself from the light, airy nothing that floated into me and turned me into a piece of paper flapping in the draught. To save my existence I would run off down the drive, for I thought I heard a voice calling. I thought I heard feet shuffling under the window, and the crunch of gravel; the click of a match being struck against a box, or a burst of male laughter.

For a long time, it seemed that it was every day for months, the operatives came with their needles and black boxes and rubber gags, and I had bad headaches afterwards and forgot where things were. But I did not forget that someone might be waiting there for me under the window.

I knew it could not be Alasdair, because he had left. He had been discharged swiftly and without question, without even his seventy-two hours' notice being demanded. The receptionist had been up and confirmed this, I remembered, bearing gladioli with a light, deft smile. So I knew it could not be Alasdair shuffling about outside. In any case he was no longer anxious about his 'performance'. He had been reassured of that by the Severn I supposed.

But I had discovered something by the Severn as well, and that is why I ran; why I sped down the cool, mulberry-green corridors with the ward-bell clanging behind me and the Italian nurse screaming:

'Phina, Phina, Josephina! Come here! Back please!'

I only wanted to be given another chance; I only wanted to walk up the hill and run down the other side to the river and capture what it was that had slipped through my fingers – whether it was love, or whether it was only physical closeness and warmth that kept this lightness out.

I never got there though. The officials in charge of the station always interjected at the mouth of the passage and barred the way, pointing gleefully to the bolted door.

'Locked! The door's kept locked, dear!' they shouted as though I were deaf, and pushed me back up the ward, like a piece of furniture being shifted, while the older women came to the doors to watch the spectacle of the stiff, jerking bundle being slid along the shiny lino.

'Play the game, Josephine,' they would cry. 'Keep the rules and you'll get well!'

As if I wanted to get well for a game that was unreal from its inception; in a waste. As if I wanted anything except to be out there and recapture the one time that I had existed!

It was a certain Wednesday, the day they high-dusted in the dormitory and went through the drawers with a basin and sponge. I was sitting on the bed among a pile of things. They were down on their knees beside the locker.

'Catch!' they called. 'Wake up! Hold this!' They were piling my possessions round me. I was almost up to my elbows in things.

The electric polisher moaned. The feather duster fluttered up and down. A wet rag had been thrust into my hand, and water trickled through between my fingers as I sat there receiving the contents of my locker.

'Coming up!' they would call as things came tumbling

up. I gazed at the strange, meaningless objects as they emerged: clothes, paper, a book, a packet of liquorice allsorts, stockings, the cap of a pen: a heap of meaningless things, as meaningless as if they had been a wheel, the front of a fire-grate, the carburettor of an engine, or a dozen lids.

'Catch!' they kept crying as they tossed. 'Catch, butterfingers!' while a little spurt of wet from the cloth I was clutching ran down my leg.

'You haven't opened your letter!' they exclaimed, examining it. It was a fat, square envelope, as white as snow. It must be the invitation to Waterminster Place. I smiled as I thought of Helena and Tony; I supposed they were *jeunes mariés* now, surrounded by their wedding trays and baskets and toast-racks and fruit-knives, and brown paper bags with messages stamped on them. There were so many things all tumbling together: heaps of gravel, and mounds of pen-nibs and tea-leaves, rubber-bands, and match-sticks, piles of shiny buns and dripping meat-carcasses, and tea-chests full of saw-dust and saucers, china ducks, wet newspaper, milk bottles and huge cement urns. There were so many things in the world drifting apart and together, and waiting for a heavy wind to scatter them finally for good. They floated round and round me, shifting, forming and dissolving, as I sat there clutching those particular numbers, those members that happened to be mine.

'You haven't opened your letter!' they were shouting again above the polisher.

I thought they meant the invitation that summoned me
to alight secretly (as though I had never been absent)
upon the world of men and women. I told them I was not
interested in invitations. The pile of things shifted again,
wire, screws, cardboard, cushions, plant-pots, as the
letter came flying up. I was not interested in invitations
any more, but I was curious to know what it was that had
held all those thirty people four storeys up, in that
softly-lit room where the music played. A metaphysical,
ontological question, perhaps, but one that required an
answer. What supported that room? Was it bricks or
iron, or just more rubble? It was precarious enough at
any rate, swaying there above the town, and all that
laughter. The whole thing rocked, I saw.

'Fancy not opening a letter,' they were remarking still
crouched over the locker, scraping at the corners. 'Look!
you haven't even undone it.'

I smiled and blinked at it. It was so white and black,
with large letters struck across it, big and bold; a semi-
script with Greek 'e's':

'Miss Josephine Traughton. By hand.'

The receptionist had brought it with the gladioli. I
remembered how I had snapped the stem of a red flower
and eaten it, and how it had stuck to the roof of my
mouth. The letter must have dropped to the floor with
the flowers and stayed there.

I snatched it eagerly. My hands were trembling.
My feet were kicking about among the debris. 'Open
it!' they were instructing me. Hope rose in me. I

thought I saw him coming down the drive to meet me.

Dear little thing, the letter ran,

I've had to push off for various reasons. I'm due for discharge in any case — they weren't really able to help me very much — so much for the 'deep, searching, etc...' — so I'm forced to start job-hunting. (!!) I'm missing you very much. I don't know what I would have done without you on those sterile institution lawns. Will these places ever learn!

As I have already said, you are one of the nicest girls I've ever met ('good' in the Kleinean sense). The first woman who did not leave a bad taste in my mouth! The first woman I did not see straight through! You've done me lots of good you know. I wish I could believe that I could do the same for you. But I'm afraid that if I stayed I should only spoil you, contaminate you with my rather sordid way of life . . . desiccated wretch that I am. And yours is such a secret, intense, unworldly life that I'd never forgive myself if I did.

Drop me a line from time to time and tell me how things are going. I expect you'll be leaving that power-house soon, and we'll be able to meet sometime and talk about old times, and rage (at least I will), and you'll bear with me, funny, nice, calm little thing. I shall always remember the first time I saw you sitting in that ditch!! Nice little Josephine!

Love, Alasdair.

They were still bending over the lockers a little way off. One was eating and had biscuit crumbs round her mouth. A blackbird swerved at the window with a worm dangling in its beak.

'Love-letter?' they asked, peering over the beds. 'Nice was it? Worth waiting for?'

That day I heard the voice outside more clearly. It was calling me distinctly, but it came from somewhere beyond the gravel of the drive. It seemed to be coming from the field along the ha-ha. I waited till I heard the ward-maid manœuvring her wagons of steaming tea through the door at the end of the corridor, then I broke through the enclave and rushed out.

It was cool and grey; the grass was wet under my feet, and everywhere the blackbirds were twittering and tooting round me. I was alone among them on the lawns. I danced across the beech-walk and the tennis courts to the field where we had sat. But when I got there, it was bare. There was nothing, no voice, no sound at all except the roaring of the poplars along the frontier. The poppies had gone, I noticed, and they had cut the grass back and it was short and stubbly and full of pools of light and black, like a wet beach that the sea has just left gleaming and rainbow-coloured.

The wall shimmered, white flowers stood up gleaming all round me. Something had changed; the breach between heaven and earth had suddenly been healed, I saw, and hid my eyes from the light that shone out. It was all so bright. My head was like air as I sat there in the silence among the blackbirds rocking myself to and fro, dazed and intoxicated. And even when they found me, and dragged me back to the ward I did not resist, for the path they took me over was bulging with soft pebbles of pink and mauve and saffron. The colours broke out in radiance as we passed over, and there beyond was a bridge of snow, and I knew that God was there. I dropped down ecstatically where they deposited me, penetrated and stupefied. The emptiness had suddenly been filled in; the gap was closed to, and I wanted nothing.

I sat there and gazed – perhaps it was weeks, perhaps months – at the brightness of everything; the bed-ends that reared up in jets from deep shafts of glittering coal underneath; the walls like newly-opened chestnut leaves; even the lino only needed a little water, I saw, to send it springing up, too, like fields of dark, shining spinach.

Sometimes the operative's sleeve passed over, and I saw the broad threads of tweed running in and out, up and down, in a glow of flickering greens and blues and browns that had a fire as their source. Sometimes a silver fish swam singing into my arm and I was singing for joy too, and wondering why the others were not singing at the sight of all these things.

Someone had come from the outness. 'Poor thing! Poor chick!' they murmured, and they told me how they were missing me at William Street, and hoped I would soon be on my feet again and back. ————

'We didn't realize exactly how solitary you were getting up there in the attic all alone! Stupid of us! Very foolish indeed! We must make amends when you get back. My daughter will probably be with us with her children during the spring. Do you like children? At least it will be someone of your own age . . . Is there anything you want in the meantime, my dear?' The mouth shifted and a cavern appeared inside, dark and stretching away. 'Is there anything Bertie and I can do for you, my dear?'

They suddenly jerked forward and sat so close and spoke so loud that I had to tell them that they might interfere with my sheets. You see between each down and cross thread of the weave I had noticed in the enclosure where the fibres intersected, a trembling violet cushion of wind was caught. A delicate, pale wind, and if they came too near they were in danger of dislodging it. If they spoke too loud, they might drive it away.

'Poor chick! Poor lamb!' they were saying. As if I were poor, I who had seen all this. As if I wanted anything!

I leaned back and let the words flow over me — like flickers on the cinema screen — and examined the boundlessly beautiful shafts of brown and cream and purple that composed the wooden arm of the chair.

Chapter Nine

THEY SAY that all happiness stops fairly soon. At least, this one did, for about Christmas a crack had opened that took away the view, and left me helping to shake out the piles of dusty crêpe paper and tinsel, and pinning up the loops and bows and puffs that were our quota of ward decorations. These things seemed to have won their victory, for there was nothing left of the other; not the strong dark of the River Severn; nor the overwhelming brightness of things that broke out after. I was left standing on a ladder calling for Scotch-tape and drawing-pins, cool and clear, without any illusions.

I think actually that Christmas was over, that it was already February and I was helping to knit jumpers for the occupational-therapy sale, and writing the tickets that announced: 'strong plastic bags' and 'a small deposit secures any article', while Dr. Clements, the Superintendent, looked over my shoulder approvingly.

It was his weekly ward-round, when he visited each patient and discussed their progress with his colleagues.

'Well?' he smiled. He was a tall, masterful man who always looked you in the eyes, unflinchingly, and read the Lesson from Corinthians at Christmas in a clear voice that resounded down the chapel. 'Well?' he smiled inquiringly.

I smiled. 'Much better these days, thank you,' and went on with my work. You see, I had found a comportment for sitting out those long days on the ward. I had found the profile that gave you parole and the right to wander from the lino to the grass and fresh air.

Not that I wanted to go very far. There was no one calling, neither God nor man, out there. It was just that a walk made 'a break' from the magazines, the knitting, the endless cups of tea, and the great warm pads of time between breakfast and lunch, tea and supper. Yes, it made time 'go nicely', as they would say, to walk up and down the cinder paths. I had no wish to go farther.

I had the profile well. I attended the Friday evening 'hops' when the band comes from the Winter Gardens, and the Sunday evening sing-songs with the Matron at the piano, and there was a certain bright, open smile which I was smiling now as the Superintendent looked down approvingly and remarked:

'Keep it up! The corners are being rubbed off nicely.' It was a laurel of paper and wool and rubber-bands that was being awarded to me.

I had acquired insight too, that most important gift, that makes you wise about your illness and your particular forms of vulnerability. It makes you as tolerant of yourself as you would be of a 'game' leg, and it comes quite naturally after a bit.

But then you learn the comportment too well, and forget that there was ever anything but this world of little things. The marks that go down on the score-board of the report-book are for the activities that are blotting out your memories.

I had grown rather fat over the last few months, sitting there with insight among the coloured wools, or at the card-table letting the cards be pulled through my fingers while the older women called out:

'Wake up, love! You've got the picture cards! Put them out, there's a love.'

I learned to put them out, but that gesture seemed to dismiss the end of the summer as though it were a fact that had only accidentally slipped into my biography at all. It was not I who had sat with Alasdair by the ha-ha and went with him earnestly and hopefully to the River Severn. That was all a misunderstanding. I was the one who sat here in the day-room with insight, understanding myself too well to wish to cling to anything.

Of course I had wanted Alasdair. I was assured of that by those who looked after me during the months that followed. That was natural; that was only to be expected. It was indeed part of the clinical picture, and tended to happen when you were recovering from an illness of this particular kind. The authorities understood only too well that feelings that have been dulled or deadened or never properly awakened, tend to raise their heads inappropriately, and very easily become unmanageable. That was a perfectly respectable phase on the road back to health, they told me, and just what was to be expected at this particular stage of my recovery . . . this indiscriminate attaching of oneself to the first object that presents itself, irrespective of real interest and mutual respect. This over-response to an emotional situation . . . Dr. Clements took it all in his stride. I was learning to feel, he patted me on the shoulder and smiled as he closed the interview. The corners were beginning to be rubbed off; I was learning to manage my experiences, and that was all that really mattered.

It was of course true, as he said, that I had not loved Alasdair any more than he had loved me. It was simply as I explained to myself over and over again, at the card-table in the day-room, or sitting by my locker in the dormitory, or perched on the high window-sill in the washrooms, that I had 'gone it too fast', had tried to rehabilitate myself all of a rush before I was quite well. 'Subtle, difficult things, these human relationships'. Dr. Clements had grimaced comically as he reminded me.

What I had conveniently forgotten was that for a moment during that week in September, something had presented itself to my mind hugely real, like a land sighted from the sea, and that I had had for a moment a sense of existing powerfully. I could stretch out and touch and share things. I could shout out across the disturbing world and someone would reply.

This I had forgotten. Not the facts of course. They were clear and vivid: the party, and the intensity of the evenings that followed. I had not even forgotten the expression on the receptionist's face as she brought me the note and the flowers, or my mad rush back to the town in a bid for self-preservation.

No, I had not forgotten anything, but I had fitted them into places that disposed of their significance and their uncomfortableness. These memories no longer counted, so I had ceased to mind. I only giggled when I thought of my wanderings, or my encounter with the man at the 'Bull'. These were things that tended to happen when you were psychologically not quite well. As the Sister had made a point of reminding me that first night in my new room upstairs, 'You would not be ashamed if you had something wrong with your leg or your arm'. So you see, I was not ashamed; the episodes were not mine. Their relevance became clear and small. And as for Alasdair and the trick that had been played on me: I did not think about them at all.

I had grown rather fat, and in front of the washroom mirror I giggled. For there was the grey skirt and pink jumper strapped about me, and the shoes bolted on. And above them was the face, heavy, puffy, quilted; the eyes too small and almost sealed down in the eyelids; the expression blank and shut-down. 'Dead-pan' Alasdair had described it. So I would giggle and then feel vaguely

sad that I could only giggle and eat too much and knit
cardigans and follow the routine of little things that kept
the momentous ones out.

'Well, you are learning to come to terms with yourself,'
Dr. Clements was saying, 'you're doing fine! Splendid!
Keep it up!'

He usually turned at this point and strode on to the
next patient, talking to his colleagues of the new Mental
Health Act or the proposed extension of the north wing.
But today he stopped where he was.

'Well, I suppose we must get you ticking over again,
eh?' he remarked. 'Our team must get to work on you,
madam. How do you feel about going back to your
work?'

'And back to my room?' I was doubtful.

'Well, I suppose the two *do* go together, don't they,
Nurse? Provided you get out and about and don't spend
all your time sitting on your bed, eh? I'll be seeing Sister
Schwarz about getting you moved back upstairs. All
right?'

I suddenly remembered about the regrading and how it
had all started.

'And what about regrading?' I asked. 'What about
schizophrenia?'

'Eh?' He came a little closer, thrust his chin out and
was jocular. 'What about it, madam?'

'I mean, is the outcome favourable?'

'That word,' he took a deep breath, 'that name is just
a label we give to a very large number of emotional

disturbances, and you know,' he smiled and lowered his voice confidentially, flatteringly, 'it is sometimes a puzzle to know what the various syndromes have in common with each other. So you see . . . ' he gesticulated to complete his thoughts and turned away. 'Well, Mrs. Webley,' he never forgot a patient's name, 'how are we?'

But I was not to be done out of the truth so easily. 'Are these illnesses curable? I mean permanently?' I persisted.

He frowned and came back towards me and put his head on one side and stared thoughtfully. 'If you stabilize by the time you are thirty . . . '

'And shall I?'

He tapped at the insides of his pockets for a moment while he thought.

'You're going splendidly,' he declared at last. 'Keep it up! If you were a "dyed-in-the-blood" we would not have got you through this little setback so well. If you were a "dyed-in-the-blood" you would never have been able even to make any contact at all with Mr. er . . . Our team has the highest hopes, I assure you. We'll have you out of here in no time! Well, Mrs. Webley, and how's Mrs. Webley? It makes you miserable, the thought of being here? Why, I've been here twenty years almost, and it doesn't make me miserable, not in the least!'

The Consultant's party trailed on with titters of laughter.

So I would go back to the top floor of the Colonel's, and look down on William Street, only without any expectations, and he would put his head round the door and say sheepishly:

'Ah well? Ah well...'

And his wife would come and stand in the doorway, with her hair flying, and implore me to come downstairs, or introduce her married daughter and I would struggle to find the right things to say to this young woman of my own age. In a handful of years ... I would stabilize or I wouldn't. If I did, I thought, I would become a rubberized old woman, immune to all hope and fear and illusion – I seemed to have developed a kind of resistance to them all – and if I didn't ...

The long ward with its double row of chipped black beds; the plastic pots underneath, the smell of urine and warm bedding and dead skin; the lino worn brown with the numbers of things and people that had been dragged over it – it was a bleak picture, but only to the uninformed. Some actually chose to stay there and refused ever to leave it because it disguised everything so well. It was not so beautiful a world as the strange bright one that had been thrust on me for a moment, but it was better than the Colonel's. It was surely better to sit there among the raffia and half-made rugs and broken lockers than to be plunged back into a world that you do not really know anything about. If you shout into a wood and do not get any reply except the echo of your own voice, you do not shout again. You give up. I would 'stabilize' or I wouldn't. It was not of much consequence either way.

Dr. Clements was half-way down the ward and Kathie was standing there, blocking his path, breathing heavily. She stood there in her sizzling chemical green dress that had been made in the O.T. hut from a teenage pattern. She was an enormous dark woman, and she stood there as she always did, folding her arms and asking the same question about her discharge.

Today she was frowning heavily. Her arms fell to her sides as she heard the Doctor's mechanical, firm refusal.

'You are under certificate,' he reminded her gently.

She roared and swore. She accused him of suppressing appeals and denying relatives and lawyers access to the hospital, while he carefully extracted a hair from his pen-nib, unperturbed, and waited. Finally he pocketed his pen and stood watching the contortions of her hairy mouth and her thick, coarse body, his head on one side, thoughtfully.

'You're going to have the operation soon,' he said quietly, 'a lobotomy, and then you'll feel better. In the meantime,' he beckoned to the nurses, who seemed to come forward with too much alacrity, 'I think we must give you some treatment.'

I watched her being dragged across the room by the armpits, grunting, writhing and struggling with stertorous snorts of fear to the nearest bed. The Doctor's face was cold and impassive as he watched them lay her out and lie across her. The black box was fetched and the apparatus was put round her head. He switched the button and a strong current of electricity flowed through her head.

'Poor Kathie,' he murmured without malice as she convulsed, gurgled and was quiet for the first time that day. 'Her troubles will soon be over.'

The Doctor's party had disappeared and I watched her coming round. Her great bulk of flesh stirred a little. Her eyes opened. She lay there half-conscious, blowing bubbles of saliva through the gag. She shifted a little, rolled her head round, grunted, and lay still and awake. A little later she dragged herself slowly on to her elbow and tried to clear her head and reorientate herself. She gave a final throaty grunt.

'I'll get my lawyers,' she whispered hoarsely. 'You won't half get it.' But her indignation was only a matter of form. She had long ago learned how she stood and she was no more outraged than Dr. Clements had been. The young nurses came forward and pulled her to her feet laughing.

'Come along Kathie! All over now! You *did* do it high that time,' they carolled, giving her a slap on the seat. 'You *did* do it high that time! Up!'

She obeyed the order and staggered to her feet, drunken and reeling, and watched with meekness her thick, brown stockings sliding to the floor.

'The suspenders have snapped,' she giggled, 'in the high jump.' She started to regather them in her thick, fumbling fingers; stopped to watch the urine dripping down her legs.

'Naughty, naughty,' the nurse wagged a finger. 'Big girl now.' She swished a swab over the pool with her foot. 'Feeling better? You'll feel much better after the op.'

Someone went over, a tall, anxious-looking woman, a newcomer perhaps, and touched her kindly and tried to help her. But Kathie only brushed her aside and stood there without a smile or a frown, in her girlish green dress, rubbing her sore parts, examining her bruises and rigging up her stockings, acquiescent. She asked for no sympathy. It had not been her fault or anyone's she knew, and so she bore them no malice.

'Did it pretty high that time,' she croaked dully as she trailed her way down the corridor. 'I've just had the treatment,' she explained. 'My head isn't half feeling bad.'

I had watched scenes like this often before, but that day it struck me differently, and I crept out into the gardens for the first time outraged. It must have been Alasdair who gave me this anger. Perhaps he had bequeathed it instead of love.

It was cold outside, and when I stood under the beech trees and heard the sounds of music coming from the recreation room I remembered that it was the *Titanic* going down. There they all were, old ladies in print pinafores and pink hair-ribbons, old men in carpet slippers slunk back against the walls, while the social workers shuffled them about, dragging them to their feet to do the 'Conga' and the 'Hokey-Cokey', shouting:

'Come along Mr. Maxton, don't leave the ladies in the field alone. Show them what the men can do.'

Here I was, a patient too, and the only thing to do was to rub the bruises with a smile, like Kathie, and get on with the knitting for the O.T. sale.

'Neural zones', 'patterns of thinking', 'brain-chemistry' . . . Insight was extinguishing me. It was that that was making me grow fat; it was that that made me giggle instead of weep.

The music struck up again, and as I heard the social workers' shouts and the obedient shuffling of many feet, and thought of coming to terms with my existence, it seemed that something was coming out of that room to destroy me.

There was before me the Mayburys, and then some other place, safe and quiet, not making too many 'emotional demands' or bringing me into contact with anything that might remind me that I was alive. It was death. I was being smothered to death.

All round me there was someone weeping. It came down on me from all sides. They were weeping very hard and my hands were wet with their tears. I shook them and cried louder:

'I was born for something else. I was born for life, for joy, for . . .' But it was not true.

I stuck my teeth into the dusty, smooth bark of the tree. I ran my mouth up and down it searchingly, and cried and cried: 'I am alive, aren't I? Aren't I, even if I don't know the rules.' I appealed, and cried more because there was no answer.

It was pure self-pity, but it was good, because when I

took my tongue away from the sour green mould of the tree, it was all quiet and silent round me as it had been that first day when the Sister had left me in the new room. My tears had purged me and my taste for life had come back.

It was cold, very, for it was February. The snow came sometimes, and yet there was no snow because a master-wind blew it all into heaps in corners that smelt of ice when the wind came off them. The air was stiff and painful, like a grazed wound that can't bleed; like a grief where there are no tears. For a moment the sun came out, and the snow-heaps had a grey-blue shadow, a bloom on them that was not snow, but the shadow of spring.

I walked across the lawns to the ha-ha. It was five months, I supposed, since we had been there last. There were dead stalks lying everywhere, and broken twigs that had burst from the trees, and Alasdair had been right about the wall that had bounded the settlement. The contractor had been there; a board had been put up, and a piece of the old grey stone had already been pulled out along the top. There was a gap, torn and white and powdery with the wind blowing fine bits of grit off.

I climbed up and peered out, but there was nothing great to see beyond. On the other side there were just fields scattered with large cold flints, a fallen tree-trunk, and cattle moving cautiously about the earth. One breathed near me wrestling with a piece of winter root, and an antique aeroplane hovered and practised overhead.

The world shrank as I watched it floating up and down.

I stood there leaning against the crumbling pile of stone and powder, and the world seemed to shrink to a little floating ball, a green sail flapping in an evening wind. And life! what a chance, what a fluke it was!

There were the animals, my friends the animals, stalking down the glades or sitting on lonely sands; swinging their tails, raising their prickles, or extending their claws. Some were sleek and white and purring, some spotted or quilled, some hard and bony with scales, and there among them within the stockade, perched precariously on the carpet called civilization with wallet and fruit-knife and vita-tabs were Helena and Tony, Alasdair, the Mayburys, and myself, while Julia's Fugitive Snakes coiled round and round the trees in ancient circles, and the peacock opened its tail with leisurely ease.

It was all absurd, but in the comedy it was we who were the clowns, the bastards, all along, so there was no time to lament one's oddness or to bother about anything but the strange thing called life that was here and now.

The narrow little room like a cupboard where I had first realized my existence was waiting for me upstairs with the window-sill so broad that you could sit there for hours looking out on to the drive and the people and the beds of lolling geraniums. It was there, waiting to have me back, but I was not tempted.

There would be the tap at the door in the evening and the kind, passionate German Sister Schwarz would be there clutching some sweetmeat under her apron, and smiling hesitantly.

'So,' she would come up and clasp me and cry. 'So! the wanderer is home again, and I am glad to see my friend that I have so missed!'

She would sit down, and in the course of our talk would remind me that mental illness is just like bodily illness, forgetting that the mind is not at all like the body, but the very opposite. There she would sit, warm and overflowing with those little condoling, cajoling acts of love to keep me resigned and contented with a certain way of life.

But I turned it down. For nothing in the jungle is ordained. The future was a blank to do what I could with. Who knew what possibility it held?

If you could stay away for fourteen days, I remembered Alasdair had told me, they could not reclaim you, so I climbed over the pile of rubble that had been my wall and had enclosed my world, said good-bye to the hill, and ran and ran until I knew for certain that I had not after all been extinguished, and that my existence had been saved.

Lightning Source UK Ltd.
Milton Keynes UK
UKOW021428041212

203162UK00011B/1000/P